Vietnam War
UPDATED EDITION

MAURICE ISSERMAN

JOHN S. BOWMAN
GENERAL EDITOR

Facts On File, Inc.

Note on Photos
Many of the illustrations and photographs used in this book are old,
historical images. The quality of the prints is not always up to modern
standards, as in some cases the originals are damaged. The content of the illustrations,
however, made their inclusion important despite problems in reproduction.

Vietnam War, Updated Edition
Copyright © 2003, 1992 by Maurice Isserman
Maps copyright © 2003 by Facts On File

Facts On File, Inc.
132 West 31st Street
New York NY 10001

Library of Congress Cataloging-in-Publication Data
Isserman, Maurice.
Vietnam War / by Maurice Isserman.—Updated ed.
p. cm. — (America at war)
Includes bibliographical references and index.
ISBN 0-8160-4937-8
1. Vietnamese Conflict, 1961–1975. I. Title. II. Series.
DS557.7 .I87 2003
959.704'3—dc21   2002008762

Facts On File books are available at special discounts when purchased in bulk quanti-
ties for businesses, associations, institutions, or sales promotions. Please call our
Special Sales Department in New York at (212) 967-8800 or (800) 322-8755.

You can find Facts On File on the World Wide Web at http://www.factsonfile.com

Text design by Erika K. Arroyo
Logo design by Smart Graphics
Maps by Jeremy Eagle

Printed in the United States of America

MP FOF 10 9 8 7 6 5 4 3 2 1

This book is printed on acid-free paper.

Contents

Preface

"Wars generate their own momentum," Robert McNamara wrote in 1995, "and follow the law of unanticipated consequences." As secretary of defense from 1961 through 1967 under Presidents John F. Kennedy and Lyndon Johnson, McNamara had been deeply involved in the decisions that drew the United States into full-scale war in Vietnam—so much so that the conflict was sometimes referred to in those years as "McNamara's War." Thirty years on, he announced in his memoir, *In Retrospect,* that he had come to the realization that he and his fellow policy makers in Washington, D.C., had been "wrong, terribly wrong," in the assumptions that guided their decision-making in the 1960s.

McNamara's belated revelation of his second thoughts about the war provoked furious controversy in the late 1990s. But he was surely right about "the law of unanticipated consequences." Among the consequences of the Vietnam War that none of its principal architects had foreseen in the early 1960s was the way in which it was destined to remain, decades after its conclusion, a source of bitter feelings and division among Americans. That bitterness and those divisions were still evident when the first edition of this Facts On File history of the war was published in 1992; they remained a part of American life a decade later, notwithstanding the dramatic changes that took place in the world later in the 1990s and at the start of the new millennium. As Arnold Isaacs, a former war correspondent, noted in his 1997 book, *Vietnam Shadows: The War, Its Ghosts and Its Legacy:* "It has been over for a generation, and the Cold War world that shaped U.S. policy has itself passed into history, but the Vietnam War still casts long shadows over American life. It lingers in the national memory, hovering over our politics, our culture, and our long, unfinished debate over who we are and what we believe."

It should be remembered that Vietnam, as a Vietnamese diplomat reminded another American reporter in 1999, "is a country not a war." The Socialist Republic of Vietnam (SRV) is, in fact, a very large country, one that in the 1990s counted 75 million inhabitants—making it the second most populous nation in Southeast Asia (after Indonesia), and the 13th most populous in the world. The majority of those 75 million people are young, having been born since 1975, the year that ended what in Vietnam is called "the American War."

In the 10 years since the first edition of this book was published, Americans have begun to reestablish long-severed contacts with Vietnam. In 1994, under President Bill Clinton, the United States lifted the trade embargo against Vietnam that had been in place since 1975. The following year, the United States extended diplomatic recognition to the SRV. In 1997, Douglas "Pete" Peterson, a U.S. Air Force pilot who was shot down over North Vietnam in 1966 and held prisoner in the notorious "Hanoi Hilton" prison camp until 1973, returned to Hanoi as U.S. ambassador to the SRV. Finally, in November 2000, President Clinton visited Vietnam, the first U.S. president to do so since the war. He received an enthusiastic reception from tens of thousands of ordinary Vietnamese citizens in the streets of Hanoi and Ho Chi Minh City (formerly known as Saigon).

Since the 1980s, the Vietnamese government has begun to open up the country to foreign investment and has actively sought foreign trade; the SRV joined the Association of Southeast Asian Nations (ASEAN) in 1996 and aspires to join the World Trade Organization (WTO), as its sometime ally, sometime enemy, the People's Republic of China, did in 2001. Meanwhile, tens of thousands of American tourists have traveled to Vietnam in recent years. Some of them are Vietnam veterans revisiting the battlefields of their youth; others are young people born since the war, looking for insight into the troubled relationship of the United States and Vietnam, or simply looking for a good time. (The appearance in the mid-1990s of a *Let's Go* budget travel guide to Southeast Asia, complete with recommendations as to the best karaoke bars in Hanoi, is suggestive of how far this latter trend has developed.)

For all the changes in U.S.-SRV relations since the early 1990s, it remains difficult for Americans, especially those of the baby boom generation or older, to think of the word *Vietnam* without immediately linking it to the word *war*. But Americans' understanding of the war has begun to change as historians and others looking back on the war have

PREFACE

developed new ways of explaining how and why that war was fought, and why it turned out the way it did. The end of the cold war and the normalization of relations with the SRV have been of immense importance in making this reinterpretation possible.

The value of the new contacts between the United States and the SRV is evident in Gen. Harold G. Moore and Joseph Galloway's 1992 memoir/history, *We Were Soldiers Once and Young* (the book that in 2002 inspired Hollywood's Vietnam war epic *We Were Soldiers*). *We Were Soldiers Once and Young* tells the story of the battle of the Ia Drang Valley (November 11–17, 1965), the first significant encounter between American and North Vietnamese soldiers in the Vietnam War. As an army colonel in 1965, Moore commanded the first battalion of the Seventh Cavalry (helicopter-borne or "airmobile" troops) in that battle; his coauthor, Joe Galloway, had been there, too, but as a young war correspondent. In researching their book, Moore and Galloway returned to Vietnam in 1990, where they interviewed Senior General Vo Nguyen Giap, the master strategist of the Communist war effort in Vietnam, and other veterans of the People's Army of Vietnam (PAVN, the North Vietnamese army). One of these officers, Hoang Phuong, now chief of the Institute of Military History in Hanoi and in 1965 a PAVN colonel who led his soldiers into battle against Colonel Moore's troopers, explained in *We Were Soldiers Once and Young* why the North Vietnamese regarded the Ia Drang battle as a victory for their side, even though they suffered heavy casualties in the fray: "Our problem was that we had never fought Americans before and we had no experience fighting them. We wanted to draw American units into combat for purposes of learning how to fight them. We wanted any American combat troops; we didn't care which ones." Moore and Galloway celebrate the heroism of the American troops in the Ia Drang Valley battle, but they acknowledge too the skill and determination of their foe, writing in the prologue to their book that "this story also stands as tribute to the hundreds of young men of the 320th, thirty-third, and sixty-sixth Regiments of the People's Army of Vietnam who died by our hand in that place. . . . They were a worthy enemy."

Former defense secretary Robert McNamara made several trips of his own to Hanoi after 1995 to meet with General Giap and other North Vietnamese military and political leaders from the war, as well as American and Vietnamese scholars studying the conflict. Along with several other authors, McNamara reported on the substance of these meetings in *Argument Without End: In Search of Answers to the Vietnam Tragedy*, published in 1999. Among the conclusions offered by the authors was the observation that "Hanoi in and of itself was never a strategic threat to Indochina; neither did it intend to be a pawn used by China to knock over the dominoes in Indochina. U.S. leaders, however, tended to see their interests in Vietnam in a larger context dominated by the Cold War struggle between the United States and the Soviet Union. . . . The American obsession with the global chessboard of the Cold War blinded leaders in Washington to the decisive importance of Vietnamese nationalism and the desire of the Vietnamese people for reunification."

The end of the cold war also made possible a new understanding of the role of the Soviet Union in the Vietnam conflict, as diplomatic archives and other sources in Moscow became available to researchers. William Duiker, a historian who served with the U.S. foreign service in Saigon in the 1960s, drew heavily on newly available sources from the archives of the Communist International (the federation of world Communist Parties that was based in Moscow in the 1920s and 1930s) in his biography, *Ho Chi Minh, A Life*, published in 2000. Among the revelations in Duiker's biography of the founder of Vietnamese communism is the fact that the Soviet Union had little interest in Vietnam in and of itself, always viewing it as a sideshow to more important struggles on the Asian continent. Soviet leader Joseph Stalin distrusted Ho Chi Minh from the 1920s on, fearing that he was more of a nationalist than a true communist. Similarly, Russian historian Ilya V. Gaiduk, drawing upon Soviet diplomatic archives to write his 1996 book, *The Soviet Union and the Vietnam War*, argued that Soviet leaders did not share Ho Chi Minh's hopes for reunification of North and South Vietnam after the Geneva Accords of 1954 had provided for the temporary division of the country into two zones. Only after the Tonkin Gulf affair in August 1964, when the United States launched its first air attack against North Vietnam, did Soviet leaders decide that, in the interests of maintaining the international balance of power (plus their own prestige within the international communist movement), they had to pull out the stops in providing aid to the North Vietnamese. Far from being mere puppets of the Soviet Union, the leaders of North Vietnam repeatedly angered their patrons in Moscow by their unwillingness to follow Soviet advice on how to pursue negotiations with the United States during the war.

PREFACE

Historians of the Vietnam War have also gained access to some important new sources from the American side. For example, in 1997 Michael Beschloss published a collection of transcripts of President Lyndon Johnson's telephone conversations in the first year of his presidency, entitled *Taking Charge: The Johnson White House Tapes, 1963–1964.* The tapes of these conversations reveal a president far less confident of the path he was charting in Vietnam than previous accounts have suggested. President Johnson sought out and received advice on Vietnam from many sources, and much of what he was hearing contradicted the official policy of steadfast support for the anticommunist cause in South Vietnam. Beschloss's book included transcripts of a number of conversations that Johnson had with Senator Richard Russell of Georgia, the influential chairman of the Senate Armed Forces Committee and one of Johnson's closest friends in Washington. Although a resolute conservative and anticommunist, Russell was dead set against the trend toward a deepening U.S. involvement in the Vietnam War. "We should get out" of Vietnam, Russell told Johnson on December 7, 1963, just two weeks after John F. Kennedy's assassination catapulted the vice president into the White House. Russell reminded Johnson of how both of them had met with President Dwight Eisenhower in 1954 and urged him not to provide direct military assistance to the French forces then fighting in Vietnam. "I tried my best to keep them from going into Laos and Vietnam as you—you were there, of course—last meeting we had under Eisenhower before we went in there. Said we'd never get out, be in there fifty years from now."

Six months later, in mid-1964, Russell again warned Johnson of the dangers of letting the United States get even more deeply involved in Vietnam than it already was: "It's a tragic situation. It's just one of those places where you can't win. Anything that you do is wrong." Russell was particularly scathing about those who were advising the president to launch air strikes against North Vietnam, a strategy that he characterized as "Bomb the North, and kill old men, women and children." He had no faith in the ability of American air power to cut off North Vietnamese support for the insurgency in the South: "We tried it in Korea. We even got a lot of old B-29s to increase the bomb load and sent 'em over there and just dropped millions and millions of bombs, day and night, and in the morning, they would knock the road at night and in the morning, the damn people would be back traveling over it. . . . We never could actually interdict all their lines of communication although we had absolute control of the seas and the air, and we never did stop them. And you ain't gonna stop these people either." Johnson listened carefully to his old friend, but he was unable to stop proceeding down the road to war.

Earlier historical accounts portrayed Presidents Kennedy and Johnson striding arrogantly, almost heedlessly into the "quagmire" of Vietnam, as it was often called, blinded to the dangers by the hard-nosed advice they were receiving from their "best and brightest" advisers in the Defense Department, State Department, and National Security Council. Thanks to new sources, and the new interpretations they suggest, historians now see the U.S. decision to escalate the war in Vietnam as less an assertion of arrogant self-confidence, and more a kind of desperate gamble against unfavorable odds to salvage what were widely recognized as failing policies in Vietnam. Historian Fredrik Logevall, for example, in *Choosing War: The Lost Chance for Peace and the Escalation of War in Vietnam,* published in 1999, emphasizes that as late as mid-February 1965 there were still influential voices within the Johnson administration attempting to head off what they feared would be the disastrous consequences of expanding the Vietnam War. In a memo to the president that month, Vice President Hubert Humphrey pointed out that most opposition to the war was coming from within the ranks of the president's own party, that there was no widespread public support for escalating the war, and that a wider war would undercut the chances for achieving domestic reform goals such as the president's Great Society proposals. "Politically, it is always hard to cut losses," Humphrey wrote to his boss. "But the Johnson Administration is in a stronger position to do so than any Administration in this century. 1965 is the year of minimum political risk for the Johnson Administration. Indeed it is the first year when we can face the Vietnam problem without being preoccupied with the political repercussions from the Republican right." But Johnson overruled Humphrey and went ahead with plans to escalate the war, even though he himself had on more than one occasion in recent months expressed his own doubts about the prospects for success in Vietnam. Humphrey, like defense secretary Robert McNamara, kept his dissent quiet. In 1968, after Johnson announced he would not run for reelection, Humphrey ran as the Democratic candidate for the presidency but was fatally burdened with the public record of being a staunch supporter of what was by then (as he had predicted in 1965) a deeply unpopular war.

For many Americans, of course, the new sources and the new interpretations change nothing. The only facts that matter are that the United States lost its first war, and that more than 58,000 American lives were thrown away in the process. That is the wound to the American spirit that has never healed, and probably never will until the generation that fought (and fought over) the war has passed from the scene, and it is left to newer and younger generations to make up their own minds about what the war meant and cost.

To this end—that is, aiding readers to consider the various aspects of the war—this updated edition of *Vietnam War* offers many new features. In addition to an expanded collection of photographs and maps, and an updated and expanded further reading section at the end of the text, the reader will also find "boxes," short articles, interspersed throughout the narrative, discussing topics ranging from the critical reception of Robert McNamara's second thoughts on the war to the popularity of the Vietnam Veterans Memorial in Washington, D.C. Readers will also find a glossary at the end of the book, providing a quick reference for understanding some of the more obscure and difficult terms that appear in the text.

In one of the finest memoirs of the war, *Father, Soldier, Son* (1996), Nathaniel Tripp, a former combat platoon leader who served in the U.S. Army's First Division in 1968, told of how he worked through his initial feelings upon arriving in Vietnam of "overwhelming terror and . . . helpless incompetence" to where he and his men became as close "as kin, as family, and all that mattered was each other." As it had for many veterans, coming home to and readjusting to life in the United States after his one-year tour of duty in Vietnam proved for Lieutenant Tripp a very long and difficult struggle. In the end he made a new life for himself, and he raised three boys of his own in the woods of Vermont. "One after another," he writes in the concluding pages of the memoir, "my own three sons have discovered my old [army] fatigues and put them on, rolling up the sleeves, shirttails dragging on the ground. I might have burned the clothing or buried it long ago, but I couldn't do so any more than I could bury the ghosts of Vietnam."

With this book, readers may try on some old fatigues and see how well or ill they still fit.

1

AMERICA
AND VIETNAM

———◆〰———

Missed Opportunities

Shortly after noon on September 2, 1945, a frail
Vietnamese man with a wispy beard stood before an enormous
crowd gathered in a central square in the northern Vietnamese city of
Hanoi. It was just a few days after the end of World War II. Vietnam,
which had been a colony of France since the 19th century, had been
occupied by Japanese soldiers during the war. Now, with Japan
defeated, there was no effective government operating in Vietnam—
except for the one that some Vietnamese were trying to provide for
themselves.

The crowd of a half-million chanted "Doc Lap"—the Vietnamese
words meaning independence—until the man who stood before them
raised his hands for silence. He then leaned forward to the microphone
and began to speak in words that sounded familiar to the few Americans who were present that day. "All men are created equal," he began.
"The Creator has given us certain inviolable Rights: the right to Life, the
right to be Free, and the right to achieve Happiness."

He stopped to ask if the crowd could hear him. When they shouted
back that they could, he continued. "These immortal words are taken
from the Declaration of Independence of the United States of America
in 1776. In a larger sense this means that 'All the people on earth are
born equal; all the people have the right to live, to be happy, to be free.'"
The speaker, a man who called himself Ho Chi Minh (which means, in

Vietnamese, "He Who Enlightens"), went on to declare Vietnam a "free and independent country." He also asked that other nations respect its right to self-determination.

Ho Chi Minh was a Moscow-trained Communist who had spent years working for the Soviet Union. Yet ironically he began his proclamation of a self-governing Vietnam with the words of the American Declaration of Independence. This was only the first of the many strange and confusing circumstances that would characterize the history of American involvement in Vietnam. In fact, when Ho first launched a military struggle for an independent Vietnam, the only

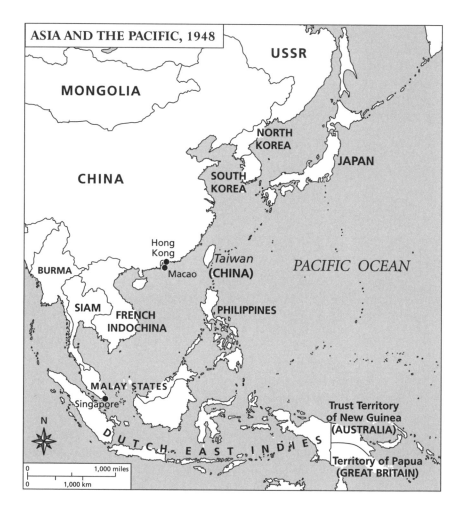

ASIA AND THE PACIFIC, 1948

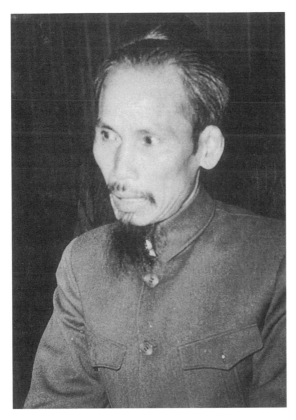

Ho Chi Minh at a political conference in Saigon, October 18, 1948 *(National Archives)*

significant amount of foreign aid he received came not from the Soviet Union but from the United States.

When countries go to war, they usually operate on the principle that "the enemy of my enemy is my friend." Thus in Europe, when the United States went to war with Nazi Germany in 1941, it logically allied itself with and provided aid to the Soviet Union, which was already fighting its own life-and-death struggle against the Nazis. It made sense for the United States to assist the resistance movements in the Nazi-occupied countries of Europe, even though some of them were led by Communists.

In the Pacific, where the United States was leading the struggle against the Japanese, it also behooved the United States to aid Communist-led resistance movements even if the long-range goals of these movements included the end of European colonial rule as well as the defeat of the Japanese. For a brief historical moment during World War II, the communist Ho Chi Minh and the capitalist United States of America needed each other, and consequently were allies.

The U.S. president, Franklin Delano Roosevelt, had little sympathy for colonialism. In August 1941 he met with the British prime minister, Winston Churchill, to draw up a list of common war aims. Roosevelt insisted that among these goals should be a pledge to "respect the right of all peoples to choose the form of government under which they will live," and to guarantee the restoration of "sovereign rights and self-government . . . to those who have been forcibly deprived of them."

Britain, like France, had its own overseas empire, and neither empire allowed its colonial subjects much say about the form of government under which they lived. Although Churchill lacked Roosevelt's enthusiasm for the principle of national self-determination, he temporarily agreed in order to keep his American ally happy. In May 1944 Churchill wrote to British foreign secretary Anthony Eden on the question of the future of the French colonial government in Southeast Asia. "Before we could bring the French officially into the Indo-China area, we should have to settle with President Roosevelt," advised Churchill. "He has been more outspoken to me on that subject than on any other Colonial matter, and I imagine it is one of his principal war aims to liberate Indo-China from France."

Roosevelt was naturally preoccupied with winning the war against Germany and Japan. He never gave any detailed thought to just how and when independence would be granted to French Indochina (which included the countries of Laos and Cambodia, as well as Vietnam). When he died in April 1945, a few months before the end of World War II, American policy in the region was still undecided. Increasingly, the U.S. State Department was leaning toward the idea of letting the French return to Indochina. This was not out of sympathy for colonialism, but in order to restore France's power and self-confidence.

The United States needed to ally with France in order to counterbalance the growing power of the Soviet Union in postwar Europe. Vietnam's lack of independence seemed a small price to pay to achieve that goal. But through September 1945 the decisions being made behind closed doors in Washington had little to do with the actions of Americans in Southeast Asia. There, military considerations were the dominant concern, leading to close relations with the Vietnamese anti-colonial forces led by Ho.

Ho Chi Minh was a shrewd man. Recognizing that the Americans were going to play a major role in shaping the postwar political situation in the Pacific region, he did all that he could to win their friendship. His followers in Vietnam were known as the Vietnamese Independence League, or "Viet Minh." They rescued American pilots who had been shot down over Vietnam while bombing Japanese ships and military installations. The Viet Minh then helped them escape to U.S. air bases across the border in China. The Viet Minh also provided valuable intelligence information on Japanese troop movements to the Americans.

In return, the U.S. Office of Strategic Services (OSS)—a wartime agency in charge of espionage and sabotage behind enemy lines—began to provide aid and advisers to Ho's forces. In July 1945 a small OSS unit parachuted behind Japanese lines in Vietnam to join up with Viet Minh forces. The OSS men found Ho deathly ill from malaria, and sent a message back to American headquarters in China requesting that a medic be sent as soon as possible. When the medic arrived two weeks later he treated the Viet Minh leader with quinine and sulfa, which probably saved his life.

For the next month the Americans trained 200 of Ho's ragged followers in guerrilla tactics. The Americans also showed them how to use the modern weapons, including mortars, machine guns, and bazookas, that had been parachuted in with them. After several weeks of hard jungle fighting against the Japanese in the late summer of 1945, the Americans accompanied the men they had trained on their triumphant march into Hanoi. Some of the Viet Minh fighters trained by the OSS would rise to top leadership positions in the Vietnamese Communist army in the next few years.

Another OSS officer, Maj. Archimedes Patti, had flown into Hanoi just after the Japanese surrender to look after liberated American prisoners of war. On August 30 Patti received a message requesting that he come to Ho's house as soon as possible. When he arrived, Ho showed him a speech, written in Vietnamese, that he intended to deliver on September 2. He asked Patti to help him polish the final version. Patti agreed, and a translator began reading the opening lines quoting the American Declaration of Independence.

According to Patti, he "turned to Ho in amazement and asked if he really intended to use it in his declaration." The young American officer had the feeling, which he later dismissed as "inane," that the words Ho planned to use belonged to the United States, and should not be used by anyone else. "Ho sat back in his chair," Patti remembered, "his palms together with fingertips touching his lips ever so lightly, as though meditating. Then with a gentle smile he asked softly, 'Should I not use it?'" Patti decided there was no good reason why Ho should not use the words. The Vietnamese leader was determined to make a gesture appealing to the American government.

As the huge crowd gathered on September 2, in Hanoi's Ba Dinh Square, Major Patti stood in an honored place on the reviewing stand next to Vo Nguyen Giap, commander of Viet Minh military forces. A Viet Minh band struck up "The Star Spangled Banner," and both Patti and Giap stood at attention and saluted. To those present, it seemed a promising start to Vietnam's independence and to future Vietnamese-American relations. Things would not be so simple.

In the southern portion of Vietnam, the Viet Minh had not been able to establish their authority as easily as in the north. Saigon, a great port city in the south, had served as the French colonial capital before the war. British soldiers arrived in September 1945 and declared a state of martial law. They clamped down on the Vietnamese independence movement, while rearming French soldiers who had been imprisoned by the Japanese. The French immediately set out to restore control of what they still regarded as their colony. Rioting broke out between the French and Vietnamese, with both sides committing atrocities against civilians. The British commander ordered Japanese soldiers, who had not yet been sent back to Japan, to help restore order, which they did by firing on crowds of Vietnamese.

A 28-year-old American OSS lieutenant colonel by the name of Peter Dewey had the bad luck to be sent by the U.S. government into this chaotic situation. Dewey was horrified by the British and French mistreatment of Vietnamese civilians in Saigon. When he tried to protest to the British commander, Maj. Douglas Gracey, Gracey at first refused to see him and then ordered him out of Saigon. On September 24, shortly before his scheduled departure, Dewey sent a message to OSS headquarters: southern Vietnam, he reported "is burning, the French and British are finished here, and we [the Americans] ought to clear out of Southeast Asia."

On the morning of September 26, Dewey packed his bags and drove out to Saigon's Tan Son Nhut airport to catch a plane to Ceylon (now

Sri Lanka). Finding his flight delayed, he tried to drive into the city for lunch. On the way back, he ran into a Viet Minh roadblock, and the Viet Minh soldiers, armed with machine guns, opened fire. Dewey slumped over dead. The Viet Minh soldiers took his jeep, and Dewey's body was never found.

It turned out to have been a case of mistaken identity. Dewey's jeep had been unmarked. (Major Gracey had refused to allow the Americans to display the American flag on their vehicles.) The Viet Minh soldiers assumed that Dewey was British or French. When Major Patti learned of Dewey's death a few hours later, he called on Ho Chi Minh in Hanoi to protest. Ho, Patti reported, was "visibly shaken" to learn of the American's death. He was afraid that it would undermine all his careful efforts to win American approval for his new government.

It really didn't make much difference. Coming soon after a war in which so many people had died, Dewey's death was considered a minor incident to all but his closest friends and associates. The United States was already turning away from any further friendly dealings with Ho Chi Minh's Communists, for reasons that had nothing to do with Major Dewey. But in dying that day in Saigon, Peter Dewey did win a small but significant place in American history. He was the first of more than 57,000 Americans fated to lose their lives in what would come to be known as the Vietnam War.

2

BACKGROUND TO AMERICA'S LONGEST WAR

Vietnam, a country of roughly 127,000 square miles (about the size of New Mexico), stretches in an S-shaped curve along the eastern seaboard of Southeast Asia. Two fertile river deltas, the Red River in the north and the Mekong River in the south, fan out to the sea. A narrow coastal plain runs up the seacoast, while a series of rugged mountain chains and high plateaus run north and south the length of the country's heavily forested interior. Much of Vietnam's long history was shaped by its geographical proximity to its giant neighbor to the north, China. In fact, the people who became known as "Vietnamese" originally migrated south from China before the beginning of recorded history. The new settlers developed an agricultural society organized around rice farming in the country's wetlands. (The region's tropical monsoon climate is ideal for the cultivation of rice, coffee, tea, and rubber.)

Vietnam's territory was first annexed by Chinese invaders about a century before the birth of Christ. China ruled Vietnam as its southernmost province for more than 1,000 years, and though Vietnam's culture, language, religion, and government were all shaped by Chinese influences, its people maintained a sense of their separate national identity. Resenting foreign domination, they repeatedly rebelled against the Chinese and other would-be rulers. In A.D. 939, a Vietnamese army defeated the Chinese and Vietnam became a separate kingdom. When the Chinese invaders returned in the 15th century they once again met

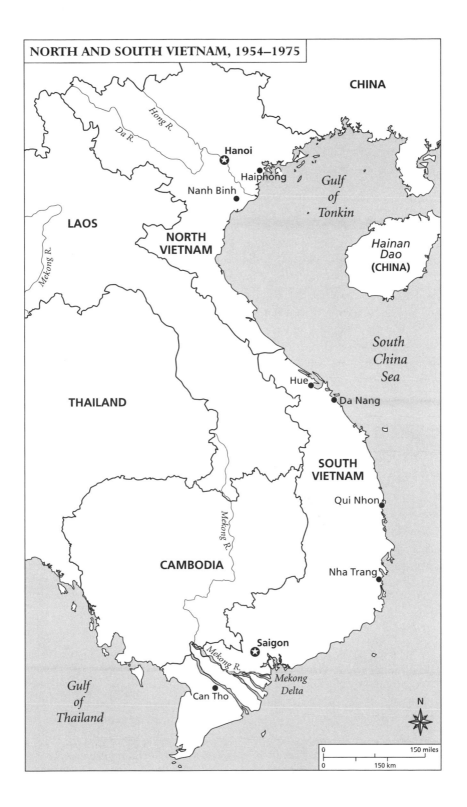

NORTH AND SOUTH VIETNAM, 1954–1975

CHINA

Hong R.

Da R.

Hanoi

Haiphong

Nanh Binh

LAOS

Gulf
of
Tonkin

NORTH
VIETNAM

Mekong R.

Hainan
Dao
(CHINA)

South
China
Sea

THAILAND

Hue

Da Nang

SOUTH
VIETNAM

Mekong R.

Qui Nhon

CAMBODIA

Nha Trang

Saigon

Gulf
of
Thailand

Mekong R.

Can Tho

Mekong
Delta

N

0   150 miles

0   150 km

determined Vietnamese resistance. The poet Nguyen Trai, who helped devise the strategy to drive off the Chinese invaders, wrote these lines to commemorate the Vietnamese victory:

> Henceforth our country is safe
> Our mountains and rivers begin life afresh
> Peace follows war as day follows night
> We have purged our shame for a thousand centuries
> We have regained tranquility for ten thousand generations.

However, victory over the Chinese did not bring permanent peace and tranquility to Vietnam. Rival family dynasties emerged in the north and south, warring with each other for centuries for control of the entire country. Long divided, the country was finally reunited at the start of the 19th century under a single emperor, Gia Long. But a new threat to Vietnamese independence soon appeared, this time coming from the west rather than the north.

This photograph from the early 20th century shows a group of 10 workers posed by palm trees in Saigon, southern Vietnam. *(Library of Congress, Prints and Photographs Division [LC-USZ62-120614])*

BACKGROUND TO AMERICA'S LONGEST WAR

The 15th century marked the beginning of a period of European expansionism, which led to the establishment of religious missions, trading settlements, and colonies in Africa and Asia, as well as to the discovery of the Americas. French Catholic missionaries arrived in Vietnam during the 17th century. Although the great majority of Vietnamese continued to practice a combination of Buddhism and Confucianism, a sizable minority were converted to the Catholic religion. Vietnamese rulers worried about the loyalty of these Catholic converts and periodically persecuted the missionaries.

In the 1850s, under the pretext of protecting its missionaries, the French set out to conquer Vietnam and convert it into a colony of France. In 1861 they captured the southern city of Saigon, and in 1863 the northern city of Hanoi. As before, the Vietnamese used guerrilla warfare tactics to harass the invaders. The rugged terrain made it difficult for foreign armies to wipe out the resistance. A French commander in southern Vietnam complained in 1862: "Rebel bands disturb the country everywhere. They appear from nowhere in large numbers, destroy everything and then disappear into nowhere." Americans would become familiar with similar complaints a century later.

By 1883 superior French military might prevailed. A treaty signed that year brought a formal end to Vietnamese independence, setting up French-controlled regional governments in the northern region known as Tonkin, the central region known as Annam, and the southern region known as Cochin China. Later, the French placed Vietnam with the other Indochinese countries it controlled, Laos and Cambodia, under the rule of a single governor. Vietnamese emperors were still allowed to sit on the imperial throne, but they were powerless to govern their people. French settlers in Vietnam gained control of the most productive farmland, throwing peasants off the land or requiring them to work as laborers on their plantations. The colonial government imposed heavy taxes on the Vietnamese, and established government monopolies trading in salt and other necessities. The government also profited from the sale of opium to the Vietnamese, leading to widespread addiction.

Although the French boasted of their *mission civilisatrice*—the "civilizing mission" of bringing the benefits of Western civilization to the people under their colonial rule—such critics as U.S. president Franklin Roosevelt remained unconvinced. Writing to U.S. secretary of state Cordell Hull early in 1944, Roosevelt expressed his dismay over the French record in the region:

France has had the country . . . for nearly one hundred years, and the
people are worse off than they were at the beginning . . . The people of
Indochina are entitled to something better than that.

Exposure to Western culture and political ideas increased native
opposition to French rule. Vietnamese students studying in French
schools in Hanoi and Saigon wondered how France could still take such
pride in 18th-century revolutionary slogans such as "Liberty, Equality,
Fraternity," while denying all three to its colonial subjects.

The European colonial empires, which grew to their greatest strength
in the 19th century, were not destined to survive the 20th century. World
War II proved to be the turning point for the British in India; the British,
French, and Belgians in Africa; and the French in Indochina. The man
most responsible for bringing an end to French colonialism in Indochina
was born in 1890, a half-century before the start of World War II, in
Nghe An province in central coastal Vietnam. As a young man he was
known as Nguyen Tat Thanh. Though well educated, Nguyen was determined to see the world, and signed onto a ship in 1912 as a common
laborer. Over the next few years he sailed to Africa, Europe, and the
United States—he lived in Brooklyn for nearly a year—and took on the
new name of Nguyen Ai-Quoc ("Nguyen the Patriot"). It would not be
until 1944 that he adopted the name by which he became best known to
history, Ho Chi Minh ("He Who Enlightens").

Ho Chi Minh did not return to Vietnam for nearly three decades, but
his country's lack of independence was never far from his mind. Ho settled in Paris during World War I. In 1919, the leaders of Great Britain,
France, and the United States met in Versailles, near Paris, to draw up the
peace treaty that would bring a formal end to the war with Germany.
U.S. president Woodrow Wilson insisted that the agreement, which
would redraw the map of Central and Eastern Europe, be based on the
principle of national self-determination. Ho Chi Minh thought that the
principles applied to the defeated empires in Central Europe should also
be applied to the overseas empires of the victorious Allies. If Czechoslo-
vakians deserved national independence, why not Vietnamese? Ho drew
up a petition calling for Vietnamese independence, and tried to present
it to the Allied leaders. No one in Versailles was interested.

Disappointed at Versailles, Ho turned elsewhere for support. In 1920
he joined the French Communist Party. Leaders of the Soviet Union,
who directed the international communist movement, called for world

revolution, including the overthrow of the colonial regimes of Asia and Africa. To Ho, the Communist movement represented a long-sought ally for Vietnamese independence: As he wrote many years later, "it was patriotism and not Communism that originally inspired me." He rose quickly within the leadership of the international communist movement, traveling to Moscow and China on its behalf.

In 1930 Ho held a secret meeting in Hong Kong to organize the Vietnamese Communist Party. However, the party could not function openly in Vietnam; Ho faced a death sentence if he was captured by the French authorities. Despite repression by the colonial government, unrest increased in Vietnam. A noncommunist nationalist group staged a revolt in 1930, put down bloodily by the French colonialists. A Communist-led revolt in several Vietnamese provinces the following year met the same fate. Most of the Communist leaders in Vietnam were arrested; Ho, still living in Hong Kong, was picked up by Chinese police and imprisoned for two years. It was not until the outbreak of World War II that Vietnamese Communists found the opportunity they had been waiting for. In 1940 France was defeated by the Nazis, and Vietnam occupied by the Japanese. Ho slipped back into Vietnam early in 1941, and formed the Vietnamese Independence Brotherhood League, or Viet Minh, to do battle with both Japan and France.

On Christmas Eve, 1944, the Viet Minh launched the Vietnamese war for independence. A small group of fighters under the command of a former history teacher named Vo Nguyen Giap attacked two French outposts, killing the officers, capturing much-needed weapons, and calling on local villagers to support the revolutionaries. Giap, a brilliant and hard-bitten Communist, whose wife had died while imprisoned by the French and whose sister-in-law had been executed by a French firing squad in Saigon, would become the master strategist of the war against the French and, later, the Americans.

The Japanese occupiers and the French colonialists had collaborated during most of the war. But in March 1945 the Japanese attacked the French colonial army, fearing it might come to the aid of an Allied invasion of Indochina. As the colonial regime collapsed, the Japanese instructed the Vietnamese emperor, a weak, luxury-loving man named Bao Dai, to declare Vietnamese "independence." Bao Dai went along with the Japanese demands, as willing to serve as a puppet for the Japanese as he had already done for the French. But the Japanese had only a few more months to give orders in Vietnam. In August, after two

With his Truman Doctrine, President Harry S. Truman pledged military and economic support to countries threatened by forces of communism or totalitarianism. *(National Archives)*

atom bombs were dropped on their home islands, the Japanese surrendered to the Allies. Ho Chi Minh seized the opportunity to make his triumphant entry into Hanoi.

Not many Vietnamese would have been sorry to see the French leave for good in 1945. Although few Vietnamese were Communists, many regarded Ho Chi Minh as the father of Vietnamese independence. The Communists reinforced their power by assassinating non-Communist rivals. Although Ho was capable of ruthless actions in pursuit of his goals, he downplayed his communist beliefs in 1945. When he addressed that crowd in Hanoi in September 1945, he still hoped that the United States would recognize his newly established government. But his hopes would soon be dashed. As far as American policy makers were concerned, Vietnam was a pawn in a much larger game.

With the defeat of Nazi Germany and Japan, the temporary wartime alliance of the United States and the Soviet Union swiftly unraveled. A "cold war" took its place, as the Soviet Union imposed a system of harsh dictatorships over the countries of Eastern Europe. American leaders were determined to block further Soviet expansion. President Harry Truman, Roosevelt's successor in the White House, told Congress on

March 12, 1947: "It must be the policy of the United States to support free peoples who are resisting attempted subjugation by armed minorities or outside pressure." In other words, the United States had to be willing to take on a new role as global policeman, prepared to step in with political or military aid any place where Communist-led movements threatened to overturn governments friendly to the United States.

With Eastern Europe firmly under the control of the Soviet Union, the United States was especially determined to shore up anticommunist governments in Western Europe, including France. Roosevelt's highly critical attitude toward French colonialism during the war seemed to policy makers in the Truman administration like a luxury they could no longer afford. If the French wanted to reestablish their empire in Indochina, the U.S. government made it clear that it would not stand in their way.

By late fall 1945, Vietnam was divided between the Viet Minh–controlled north and the French-controlled south. Negotiations dragged on for more than a year between the French and Communist forces. Ho was willing to concede the right of French troops to remain in Vietnam for another five years, in exchange for recognition of Vietnamese independence. But the French were determined to crush Ho's government as soon as possible. In November 1946 French naval forces shelled the northern port of Haiphong, killing at least 6,000 civilians. The attack marked the beginning of the first Indochinese war. The Viet Minh soon abandoned the cities, and fought back from the countryside using guerrilla tactics. The French brought the former emperor Bao Dai back from exile to head a new "independent" state that was in reality still controlled by France.

In the war that followed, the French controlled all of Vietnam's cities and enjoyed an overwhelming advantage in weaponry. In 1946 the Viet Minh military forces consisted only of lightly armed infantry; not until after 1949 did they begin receiving Chinese and Soviet weapons, including heavy artillery. The Viet Minh's great advantage was its ability to hide in Vietnam's rugged landscape and vast jungles. They also enjoyed popular support. They could move openly throughout the countryside without fear of betrayal, while every French military move was reported to the Viet Minh by local civilians. The French army was tied down defending cities and rural strong points, while the Viet Minh remained constantly on the offensive, staging small-scale but effective attacks on scattered French units and outposts.

Other armies were on the march in Asia. In 1949 the Chinese Communists drove the American-backed Nationalist forces off the Chinese mainland. In June 1950 the army of Communist North Korea invaded anticommunist South Korea. The United States, acting under the banner of the United Nations, came to the aid of the South Koreans. For the first time Americans were engaged in a full-scale shooting war against a Communist enemy. The U.S. government, fearing that all of Asia might soon be ruled by the Communists, now decided to throw its weight behind the French war effort in Indochina. On June 29, 1950, eight U.S. military transport planes flew to Vietnam delivering weapons to the beleaguered French army, the first direct American military aid to the anticommunist cause in Vietnam. Shortly afterward the United States recognized the Bao Dai administration as the legitimate government of Vietnam. Over the next few years the United States would provide $3 billion in aid to the French in Vietnam, funding 80 percent of their war effort.

The French suffered a series of military setbacks in Vietnam during the late 1940s and early 1950s. In May 1953 a new French commander, Gen. Henri Navarre, took command in Vietnam, declaring "Now we can see [military success] clearly, like light at the end of a tunnel." Seeking a showdown with the Communists, Navarre stationed 15,000 of his best troops in a remote village in northwestern Vietnam called Dien Bien Phu in the late fall of 1953. Navarre hoped to lure Viet Minh troops into an open battle where French superiority in arms could prevail. But Navarre's opponent, the self-taught military strategist General Giap, turned out to have a better grasp of the lay of the land than the French commander.

Over a period of several months, Giap's troops surrounded the isolated French base, blocking all roads for reinforcement. Civilian laborers cut a road through seemingly impassable jungles and over mountains to enable the Viet Minh to drag heavy artillery onto mountaintops overlooking Dien Bien Phu. On March 13, 1954, Giap launched his offensive. For the next two months the Viet Minh pounded the French garrison night and day with artillery and dug their trenches ever closer to French lines. The only way the French soldiers could be resupplied was by air, including missions flown by Americans in unmarked planes owned by the Central Intelligence Agency; two American pilots were shot down and killed in the effort. Heavy Viet Minh antiaircraft fire and the arrival of the monsoon rains in late March cut off most French supplies. Before Dien Bien Phu was surrendered on May 7, 1954, 5,000 French troops died.

A French foreign legionnaire walks along a rice paddy in the Red River Delta between Haiphong and Hanoi, 1954. *(National Archives)*

In Washington, the news from Dien Bien Phu had been closely monitored by government and military leaders. Adm. Arthur Radford, chairman of the Joint Chiefs of Staff, proposed to President Dwight D. Eisenhower that the U.S. launch air strikes to relieve the defenders of Dien Bien Phu, possibly including the use of tactical nuclear weapons. Several influential lawmakers, including Massachusetts senator John F. Kennedy and Texas senator Lyndon B. Johnson, warned against such intervention. Army chief of staff Matthew Ridgway also was strongly opposed. Air strikes alone would not work. And if U.S. ground forces were sent in, he warned, it might take more than 500,000 troops to win the war against the Viet Minh.

President Eisenhower, who had been elected to office in 1952 in part because of his promise to end the war in Korea, was reluctant to get involved in another costly land war in Asia. In the end he decided against aiding the defenders of Dien Bien Phu. However, he remained convinced that Vietnam's preservation as part of the "free world" was essential to U.S. security. At a press conference in April 1954 he warned: "You have a row of dominoes set up, and you knock over the first one and what will happen to the last one is the certainty that it will go over very quickly." This was the origin of what became known as the "domino theory," the idea that the fall of Vietnam would bring further Communist triumphs throughout Southeast Asia, Japan, and the Philippines, perhaps even threatening Hawaii and the American mainland in the long run.

The USS *Montague* takes aboard refugees from Haiphong in August 1954. *(National Archives)*

President Dwight D. Eisenhower speaks to the press, with his wife, Mamie Eisenhower. *(Library of Congress, Prints and Photographs Division [LC-USZ62-90397])*

In Geneva, Switzerland, one day after the fall of Dien Bien Phu, an international summit of Western and Communist powers turned to the issue of Indochina. Although Ho Chi Minh expected to take power in all of Vietnam, the French struck a deal with Ho's allies—the Soviet Union and the People's Republic of China—to force him to settle for less. The compromise agreement, known as the Agreement on the Cessation of Hostilities in Viet-Nam (Geneva accords), provided for the temporary division of Vietnam along the 17th parallel, with the Communist forces in power in the north and non-Communists in control of the south. The question of who would in the end rule over a reunified Vietnam was to be decided by an internationally supervised election in 1956, two years later. The U.S. government disapproved of any settlement turning territory over to the Communists and did not sign the Geneva accords. Over the next few months, the first small and fateful steps were taken that would eventually lead to the dispatch of hundreds of thousands of Americans to fight in South Vietnam.

3

ORIGINS OF U.S. INVOLVEMENT

1954–1961

In 1971, the *New York Times* published a secret government study of the origins of American involvement in the still-raging Vietnam War. The study, known as the Pentagon Papers, had been ordered by Secretary of Defense Robert McNamara in 1967. Only 15 copies were produced. It was never meant to be read by the public, and would not have been, had it not been for a former Defense Department official named Daniel Ellsberg. Ellsberg, who had grown disillusioned with the war, passed on a copy to reporters. Thanks to the Pentagon Papers, historians know a great deal about the attitudes and goals of the political and military leaders who led the United States into the Vietnam War. One of the most interesting conclusions that the authors of the Pentagon Papers came to was that "South Vietnam was essentially the creation of the United States." To understand what they meant requires returning to the moment in 1954 when the French empire in Indochina crumbled and Ho Chi Minh's Communists were poised to take control over all of Vietnam.

The Geneva accords provided for the temporary division of Vietnam along the 17th parallel. When the French withdrew from northern Vietnam in the fall of 1954, the Communists moved swiftly to establish their own government. Meanwhile the emperor, Bao Dai, appointed a prime minister in June 1954 to organize a government for the southern half of the country. The man he chose was Ngo Dinh Diem, a conservative nationalist from a wealthy background whose family belonged to Vietnam's minority of Catholic believers. Diem had held a number of posts in the colonial government in the 1920s and 1930s, but grew increasingly critical of French rule in those years. During the war he established contacts with the Japanese occupation forces. In 1945 the Japanese considered offering him the post of prime minister in the puppet government they were setting up in Vietnam, but they were not sure they could rely on him. After the war Diem supported the cause of Vietnam's independence, but opposed the Communists, turning down an offer from Ho Chi Minh to join the Viet Minh government in 1946. Under threat of Communist assassination, Diem fled Vietnam in 1950 to live in a Catholic seminary in the United States.

While he was in the United States, he made some influential friends, including Francis Cardinal Spellman of New York, a leading Catholic spokesman in the United States. Spellman was bitterly opposed to the Geneva settlement. He told an American Legion convention in the summer of 1954 that the agreement meant "taps for the newly betrayed millions of Indochinese who must now learn the awful facts of slavery from their eager Communist masters!" Spellman, John F. Kennedy, and other influential men regarded Diem as the man best suited to save Vietnam from Communist domination. They played an important behind-the-scenes role in influencing the United States government to back Diem when he returned to Vietnam in June 1954 to become Bao Dai's prime minister. As emperor, Bao Dai was still the official head of state in South Vietnam; he and Diem were soon at odds over how much power Diem should exercise. In October 1955, with the backing of the United States, Diem organized a national referendum that led to the creation of the new Republic of Vietnam (South Vietnam). Diem was the republic's first president. Diem kept the old Vietnamese imperial flag of three red stripes on a yellow background as his government's flag. Ho Chi Minh's Democratic Republic of Vietnam (DRV) in the north adopted the Viet Minh flag of a yellow star on a red background as its national symbol.

The Eisenhower administration, which had disapproved of the settlement made in Geneva, decided in the summer of 1954 to provide aid to South Vietnam to hold off further Communist advances. By August Eisenhower had assigned more than 300 military personnel to the U.S. Military Assistance Advisory Group (MAAG) in Vietnam. The Americans with MAAG played a key role in training, equipping, and advising the Army of the Republic of Vietnam (ARVN), the military force of Diem's South Vietnam.

Diem found another helpful friend in those early days in U.S. Air Force colonel Edward G. Lansdale. Lansdale was assigned in the summer of 1954 to direct Central Intelligence Agency (CIA) activities in Vietnam. A veteran of the fighting in the Pacific during World War II, Lansdale had also worked with the U.S.-backed government in the Philippines during the late 1940s in putting down a Communist guerrilla uprising. Lansdale was convinced that the reason the French had failed in Indochina was because they relied too heavily on conventional military tactics. When American CIA agents in Hanoi were pulled out of the city in October 1954 as the last remaining French soldiers withdrew, Lansdale reported to Washington that the Americans were

> disturbed by what they had seen of the grim efficiency of the Vietminh in their takeover, the contrast between the silent march of the victori-

President Dwight D. Eisenhower and Secretary of State John Foster Dulles (from left) greet South Vietnam's president, Ngo Dinh Diem, at Washington National Airport. *(National Archives)*

A U.S. Air Force C-47 releases psychological warfare leaflets near Nha Trang, South Vietnam. *(National Archives)*

ous Vietminh troops in their tennis shoes and the clanking armor of the well-equipped French whose western tactics and equipment had failed against the Communist military-political-economic campaign.

Lansdale, a swashbuckling figure, was determined to succeed where the French had failed. His agents in Hanoi struck what small blows they could against the new Communist regime. They poured acid into oil tanks to sabotage Hanoi's buses and tried unsuccessfully to destroy the city's printing presses. They had more success with "psywar" (psychological warfare) tactics. They printed up phony leaflets, supposedly issued by the Viet Minh, announcing harsh new policies for the confiscation of private property, spreading panic and leading to an increased flow of refugees southward. The Geneva accords had provided for the free movement of refugees north and south for a period of 300 days. During that time U.S. planes dropped propaganda leaflets on northern Vietnam proclaiming "the Virgin Mary is moving south," warning of the danger of anti-Catholic persecutions under the Communists. Some 900,000 Vietnamese fled south in 1954 to 1955, two-thirds of them

Dr. Tom Dooley and the Battle of Good and Evil in Vietnam

WHEN JOHN F. KENNEDY FIRST PROPOSED TO CREATE the Peace Corps, he cited "the selfless example of Dr. Tom Dooley." As a U.S. Navy doctor in the summer of 1954, Tom Dooley took part in the Central Intelligence Agency–organized Operation Passage to Freedom, transporting Catholic refugees from North to South Vietnam. His sensational account of this exodus, *Deliver Us from Evil,* was serialized in *Reader's Digest* and became a best-seller in the United States in 1955. Dooley's writings gave many Americans in the 1950s their first look at a place called Vietnam. However, he greatly exaggerated both his own role in the rescue operation and tales of Catholic martyrdom at the hands of the Viet Minh, contributing to a simplistic vision of the Vietnamese conflict as a place where good battled evil. Resigning from the navy in 1956 under less than honorable circumstances, Dooley opened a privately funded medical clinic in Laos, and he became a tireless publicist for the anticommunist cause in Southeast Asia. Until his death from cancer in 1960, he was widely viewed in the United States as a living example of selfless American idealism in the service of humanity.

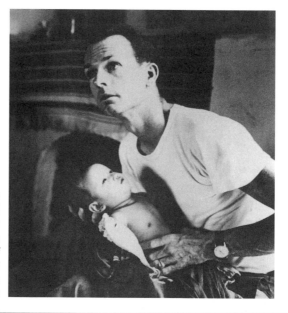

Dr. Thomas A. Dooley examines an ill child at a hospital in northern Laos in 1960. *(Library of Congress, Prints and Photographs Division [LC-USZ62-109669])*

Catholics, many of them transported south in American ships and planes; 130,000 supporters and family members of Viet Minh moved north in the same period. But 8,000 to 10,000 "stay-behinds" from the Viet Minh remained secretly in South Vietnam, the core around which Communist military forces in the south would later be rebuilt.

Lansdale forged a close personal relationship with Diem in the mid-1950s, becoming the chief U.S. adviser to the South Vietnamese government, and helping Diem consolidate his power over other anticommunist rivals in South Vietnam. With Lansdale's aid, Diem set up the referendum in 1955 on the question of whether South Vietnam should remain a monarchy under Bao Dai or become a republic under Diem. An overwhelming but obviously fake majority of 98.2 percent of the votes counted in the referendum were in favor of Diem and the republic. (In Saigon, Diem managed to receive several hundred thousand more votes than there were registered voters in the city.) Some Americans in South Vietnam, including Ambassador J. Walter Collins, developed doubts about Diem's abilities to create a stable government, but Lansdale and Diem's supporters in the United States convinced the Eisenhower administration that there was no alternative except to stick with him. By the end of the 1950s the United States had poured nearly $2 billion of aid into South Vietnam, mostly to shore up its military and police forces.

In 1956 Diem refused to hold the election called for in the Geneva accords, which would have reunified the two Vietnams under a single government. As President Eisenhower later acknowledged, if an election had been held in the country in 1956, Ho Chi Minh would have received 80 percent of the vote. The Geneva accords had declared that division between northern and southern Vietnam at the 17th parallel was "provisional and should not in any way be interpreted as constituting a political or territorial boundary." Diem made the decision not to hold the election on his own, but he could not have done it without the assurance of continued American support. When Diem visited the United States in May 1957, President Eisenhower described him as the "miracle man" of Asia, who had saved his country from communism.

In the short run, Diem was successful in preventing a Communist takeover in the south. In the north the Communists had imposed a harsh dictatorship. One of the grimmest aspects of the Communist rule was the land reform campaign of 1955 to 1956, designed to redistribute land to the poorest peasants. During the course of the campaign 10,000 to 15,000 peasant landowners, many of whom owned only a few acres of land themselves, were executed and thousands more arrested or deported. There was widespread dissatisfaction with these policies, and in Ho Chi Minh's home province the peasants rose in a brief, bloodily put-down rebellion. North Vietnamese Communists later publicly admitted "errors" in their actions, including, in the words of General Giap, the executions of "too many honest people."

In South Vietnam, Diem's policies were also undemocratic and unpopular. By 1959 his government had arrested more than 40,000 political opponents. Thousands were tortured or shot without trial. The victims included liberal, nationalist, and religious critics of Diem's regime, as well as Communists. Newspapers that criticized Diem were shut down by government orders. Under pressure from the U.S. government, Diem launched his own land reform program to secure the support of South Vietnamese peasants. But the campaign was half-hearted, ineffective, and corrupt. In fact, government officials often took back land that the Viet Minh had distributed to peasants during the war against the French, and returned it to large landowners. In 1960 three-quarters of South Vietnam's land was still owned by only 15 percent of its population. The "agroville" campaign, launched in 1959, also antagonized the peasants; villagers were forced to relocate from Communist-controlled areas of the countryside to new villages in areas controlled by the government. The policy was meant to increase support for the government, but the peasants resented being forced to leave their familiar homes and fields and the graves of their ancestors. The agroville program was abandoned in the early 1960s but replaced by an equally unpopular strategic hamlet program in 1962, in which peasants were herded into fortified villages in the countryside.

Armed resistance to the Diem regime began in the late 1950s as spontaneous acts of self-defense against government repression. In the mid-1950s North Vietnamese Communists, preoccupied with their own problems, ordered the Communist "stay-behinds" in South Vietnam to lie low. North Vietnamese leaders like General Giap argued that the Communists should concentrate on building up the economy and securing their political control of the north. Others, including Communist leaders born in South Vietnam like Le Duan, secretary-general of the Lao Dong (Communist) Party, favored a more aggressive policy, including North Vietnamese military aid to a southern war of "national liberation." The debate in the north between these two positions had not been resolved when in 1957 South Vietnamese Communists began to form small guerrilla bands to fight the Diem government.

Communist military strength was at first concentrated mostly in the western Mekong Delta, but soon extended to the Central Highlands and coastal plains. South Vietnamese Communists began assassinating local police and village officials appointed by Diem. In October 1957 Communist guerrillas set off bombs at the U.S. MAAG offices in Saigon, wounding 13 Americans. Two years later, on July 8, 1959, an American officer and an enlisted man were killed in a guerrilla attack on a MAAG compound in Bien Hoa, the first American deaths in the renewed Vietnam fighting.

In 1959 North Vietnam began for the first time to supply significant military aid to Communist guerrillas in the south. Until then the guerrillas had fought with arms left over from the war against the French or captured from the Diem government. Fighting men, as well as weapons, were also sent to the south; until 1964 most of the infiltrators were natives of the south who had moved north after the signing of the Geneva accords. This marked the beginning of the "Ho Chi Minh trail," the main Communist infiltration route that wound down from North Vietnam into Laos and from there into South Vietnam. These trails cut through deep jungles and forests and were carefully camouflaged to be invisible to air reconnaissance and attack. The journey along this series of trails could take up to two and a half months from North to South Vietnam. It was usually done on foot, though in later years thousands of trucks were also used to transport people and supplies through Laos.

As the 1950s came to an end, the war in Vietnam was still being fought at a low level of intensity, its effects largely invisible from the cities. William Colby, Central Intelligence Agency (CIA) station chief in Saigon (who would later become director of the CIA), described how the Communists spent the late 1950s carefully laying the groundwork for the revolution against the Diem regime:

> They first began the process of political organization in the villages, going through the villages giving the arguments on behalf of the continuing revolution—now not against the French but against the Americans and Diem . . . They were trying to identify the continued effort with the earlier nationalist effort . . . There were speeches, recruiting,

things of this nature, an occasional murder of a very vigorous village chief, an occasional murder of some corrupt official . . . This went on for a couple of years.

In 1960, on instructions from the north, Communists in South Vietnam organized the National Liberation Front (NLF). They adopted a flag resembling that of North Vietnam as their banner, with a yellow star in the middle of a split field of red and blue. The South Vietnamese government referred to the NLF as the "Viet Cong," which means Vietnamese Communists.

By the start of the 1960s, the fate of South Vietnam loomed large in the minds of top U.S. policy makers, but it had made little impact on the U.S. public. The key decisions committing the United States to support Diem had been made behind closed doors in Washington, with little fanfare or open debate. Until the massive escalation of the war in the mid-1960s, most Americans probably would not have been able to find Vietnam on a map. In the 1960 presidential election campaign Vietnam was hardly mentioned, although the fate of two tiny islands off the coast of Communist China, Quemoy and Matsu, was hotly argued in a televised debate between Democratic candidate John F. Kennedy and Republican candidate Richard Nixon.

When John F. Kennedy was elected president in November 1960, he inherited a policy of U.S. government involvement in Vietnam that had been fashioned by Harry Truman and Dwight Eisenhower over the previous 10 years. The country that the United States "created," South Vietnam, was an established fact. Approximately 900 U.S. military advisers were then stationed in the country, while hundreds of other Americans were running various intelligence, police, and aid programs. Kennedy could not ignore South Vietnam's existence or fate—nor did he want to. He had, after all, been one of Diem's earliest supporters in the United States. He had also just won an election over his Republican opponent, in part by charging that the Eisenhower administration had allowed the United States to "fall behind" the Russians in the cold war. In his inaugural address in January 1961 he pledged that under his leadership the United States would "pay any price, bear any burden, meet any hardship, support any friend, oppose any foe to assure the survival and success of liberty."

Kennedy, born in 1917, was the youngest man ever to have been elected president of the United States. He was part of the generation

Crowds on the east portico of the U.S. Capitol watch the inauguration of President Kennedy on January 20, 1961. *(Library of Congress, Prints and Photographs Division [LC-USA7-19598])*

that had fought in World War II; as a navy officer he commanded a PT (patrol torpedo) boat in the Pacific and had heroically rescued one of his sailors when his boat was sunk by a Japanese destroyer. Kennedy's outlook on the world had been decisively shaped by the history of the 1930s and 1940s. Because the Western democracies refused to stand up to Nazi Germany's dictator Adolf Hitler in the 1930s, Hitler's appetite for conquest had grown out of control. "Appeasement" of dictators like Hitler—and later, Stalin—did not guarantee peace; in fact, it was a recipe for wider and more dangerous conflicts. In 1957 Chinese Communist leader Mao Zedong boasted that the "East Wind" would prevail over the "West Wind," which was to say "the socialist forces are overwhelmingly superior to the imperialist forces." Mao ridiculed the United States as a "paper tiger" that could do nothing to reverse the tide of Communist victories in the world. In 1961, shortly before Kennedy was inaugurated, Soviet Communist leader Nikita Khrushchev pledged that his country would come to the aid of "wars of national liberation" around the world. Kennedy came into office determined to prove that the United States was not a paper tiger. He would not "appease" what he, like Truman and Eisenhower before him, regarded as the Communist appetite for conquest in Southeast Asia.

Vietnam also provided the new Democratic administration the opportunity to engage in what was referred to as "nation-building." Kennedy's advisers believed that in Third World countries "underdevelopment" had given the Communists an opening to stir up trouble. The United States could counter the appeal of Communism by contributing to the modernization of the societies and economies of the Third World. In other words, the more that countries like South Vietnam became like the United States, the happier their people would be, and the more securely they would become part of the "Free World."

In places like South Vietnam, Kennedy's advisers thought that it was the Americans who were the real revolutionaries, not the Communists: "Our central task in the underdeveloped areas," Kennedy adviser Walt Rostow declared in a speech to U.S. Army Special Forces troops in 1961, "is to protect the independence of the revolutionary process now going forward." The United States was not "dragged" into Vietnam; in those early days of involvement, South Vietnam promised Americans challenge and adventure. Ogden Williams, a CIA agent who worked as an assistant to Colonel Lansdale in Saigon, would later recall Vietnam as an "enormously attractive" place to Americans:

> There was that sense of a young country, which was very inspiring . . . There was a very graceful, traditional culture, an enormously pleasant way of life. Saigon was an elegant city. The beautiful tropical foliage, the flamboyant trees, the cabarets, the lovely slim women . . . The whole thing was just elegant and romantic as hell . . . It was always an enormous letdown to come back to the States.

The first months of the Kennedy administration were filled with foreign policy frustrations. In April 1961, a U.S.-sponsored invasion of Cuba by anticommunist Cuban exiles was crushed by Fidel Castro's forces. In Laos, Kennedy hesitated to commit U.S. troops to fight against the Communist-led Pathet Lao forces, agreeing instead to an international summit that set up a neutralist coalition government for the country. In Europe, Khrushchev built a wall across the divided city of

Berlin and threatened Soviet military action against West Berlin. In June 1961 when Kennedy met with Khrushchev in Geneva, the Soviet leader tried to intimidate the young American president. Shaken by the meeting, Kennedy remarked to a reporter from the *New York Times:* "Now we have a problem in making our power credible, and Vietnam is the place." The country America had "created" in the 1950s was about to draw Americans into the most destructive conflict since World War II.

4

KENNEDY'S WAR

1961–1963

In the early 1960s the United States grew ever more deeply involved in the war in Vietnam even though President John F. Kennedy never made a clear-cut decision to commit American military forces to a combat role in South Vietnam. He hoped a limited commitment of American advisers and equipment would turn the tide against the Communists. But the Viet Cong grew stronger and bolder every year. The American-backed government of Ngo Dinh Diem proved incapable of resisting the Communists and was increasingly unpopular with the people of South Vietnam. If American weapons in South Vietnamese hands were not the answer, then perhaps American weapons in American hands would have to take their place—or so some in Washington began to think.

The cold war changed its character as the 1950s ended. "In the 1940s and early fifties," Kennedy warned Americans in 1961, "the great danger was from Communist armies marching across free borders, which we saw in Korea." Now the threat took a new form, "local conflict" that Communists "can turn in their favor through guerrillas or insurgents or subversion." The nuclear superpowers, the United States and the Soviet Union, each possessed the capability to destroy the other in an all-out war. Leaders in Washington felt that this great destructive power actually tied their hands when confronted with "wars of national liberation" in the Third World. The United States could not threaten to drop an atomic bomb on Moscow or Beijing every time a band of guerrillas backed by the Soviet Union or China tried to topple some friendly government. It was simply not believable—or "credible" in the language that policy makers favored—that the United States would risk nuclear war to save a country like South Vietnam. To defeat the Communists, and thus preserve the "credibility" of American national power, the United States would have to learn to defeat guerrilla wars through a new type of military response: "counterinsurgency."

When Kennedy took office, his thinking on South Vietnam was influenced by Edward Lansdale. Lansdale gave Kennedy a situation report on Vietnam in January 1961, urging the new administration to continue its support for the Diem government. Lansdale warned the new president that the military and political situation in Vietnam was going from bad to worse. He was not exaggerating. The Viet Cong dramatically stepped up the pace of its guerrilla attacks in South Vietnam in 1961, assassinating more than 1,400 government officials and temporarily capturing the town of Phuoc Binh, a provincial capital 40 miles north of Saigon. "This is the worst one we've got, isn't it?" Kennedy remarked to an adviser when he finished reading Lansdale's report.

Kennedy was also influenced by a group of distinguished, self-confident advisers he appointed to high offices in his administration, the "best and the brightest," in the words of journalist David Halberstam. Many of Kennedy's key advisers were graduates of or teachers at top Ivy League universities, particularly Harvard University. Robert McNamara was a graduate of the Harvard Business School who had risen to the presidency of Ford Motor Company when tapped by Kennedy to serve as secretary of defense. McGeorge Bundy was dean of arts and sciences at Harvard until called to take the post of Kennedy's national security adviser. Walt W. Rostow was a professor of economics at Massachusetts Institute of Technology, until he went to Washington to serve as chairman of the State Department Policy Planning Council under Kennedy. The only top Kennedy adviser with combat experience was retired U.S. Army general Maxwell Taylor. Taylor had parachuted with his troops of the 101st Airborne Division during the invasion of Normandy in World War II. He resigned as army chief of staff in the late 1950s because of his disagreement with what he felt were the old-fashioned military policies of the Eisenhower administration. He was appointed military adviser to the Kennedy administration and in 1962 became chairman of the Joint Chiefs of Staff. These were the men who made the critical decisions leading to the United States's deepened military involvement in Vietnam.

VIETNAM WAR

President Kennedy meets with Secretary of Defense Robert McNamara in the White House Cabinet Room. *(John F. Kennedy Library)*

Kennedy was aware of the conventional wisdom that it was foolish for the United States to get involved in another land war in Asia. But he never considered abandoning the American commitment to the preservation of a non-Communist South Vietnam. Kennedy could not forget the way that the last Democratic president in the White House, Harry Truman, had been attacked in the early 1950s by Republican opponents like Wisconsin senator Joseph McCarthy for "losing" China to the Communists in 1949. As he complained privately to an aide in 1963, "If I tried to pull out completely now from Vietnam we would have another Joe McCarthy red scare on our hands." International concerns reinforced such domestic ones. Kennedy felt he had to prove to Khrushchev and Mao that the United States was not a paper tiger, that it had the will and the power to defend its interests and allies abroad—that it had, in a word, credibility.

The use of credibility as a rationale for American involvement in Vietnam was a self-fulfilling prophecy. The more the United States declared that Vietnam was the place where its credibility would be established, the more its credibility would suffer if things did not work out as expected. George Ball, who served as undersecretary of state in both the Kennedy and Johnson administrations, once warned Kennedy that deepening involvement in Vietnam could get out of hand, leading to the deployment of hundreds of thousands of American troops. Kennedy laughed, telling him, "George, you're supposed to be one of the smartest guys in town, but you're crazier than hell. That will never happen."

Kennedy's confidence was based on his faith in the new tactics of counterinsurgency. Chinese Communist leader Mao Zedong had taught his followers that in guerrilla war maintaining close relations with the local populace was all-important: The guerrillas were the fish swimming in the sea of the people. American strategists in the early 1960s reasoned that the way to defeat a guerrilla war was to dry up the sea of popular support for the guerrillas. That meant convincing the people that they should give their allegiance to the government and not the guerrillas, a strategy known as "pacification" or "winning hearts and minds."

Secretary of Defense Robert S. McNamara (left) and Gen. Maxwell D. Taylor (center), chairman of the Joint Chiefs of Staff, arrive in South Vietnam on a fact-finding mission for President Kennedy. General Paul Harkins (right) guides them through a field headquarters in Saigon, September 28, 1963. *(National Archives)*

The men of the U.S. Army Special Forces were assigned a special role in this new strategy. The Special Forces, headquartered in Fort Bragg, North Carolina, had been established in 1952 to wage unconventional warfare: fighting behind enemy lines, living off the land, and enlisting and training local populations for guerrilla operations. In Vietnam the Special Forces would find themselves used for a somewhat different purpose—fighting guerrillas with guerrilla-like tactics. The first Special Forces units had been sent to Vietnam in 1957 to train ARVN troops in counterinsurgency tactics. Kennedy believed that Special Forces represented the kind of "flexible response" capability the United States needed to counter the Communists in such places as Vietnam. He ordered their expansion and authorized them to wear the distinctive headgear that gave them their popular nickname, the "Green Berets."

By the spring of 1961, Kennedy had already sent an additional 400 Special Forces soldiers to Vietnam. The Fifth Special Forces Group was set up in September 1961 to coordinate the mission of the Green Berets in South Vietnam. They shifted their activities from training ARVN

Troops of South Vietnam's army watch training demonstration by members of U.S. military advisory group attached to their division, October 21, 1961. *(National Archives)*

Robert McNamara's Second Thoughts

IN 1995 ROBERT McNAMARA PUBLISHED A MEMOIR entitled *In Retrospect*. It had been 28 years since he had resigned as secretary of defense, at the height of the Vietnam War, to assume the presidency of the World Bank. For all those years he had remained silent about the conflict that in the early 1960s had sometimes been called "McNamara's War."

Now, in looking back on the Vietnam War, he confessed that he and his fellow policy makers in the Kennedy and Johnson administrations had "been wrong, terribly wrong." The war in Vietnam had been a civil war, not a war of foreign aggression. The enemy that the United States fought in Vietnam was motivated primarily by nationalism, not by a desire to spread communism beyond Vietnam's borders. The fall of South Vietnam posed no serious threat to U.S. security interests. American leaders, both political and military, had an unfounded faith in the power of technologically sophisticated weaponry to counter a popular guerrilla war. The United States could and should have withdrawn from South Vietnam in 1963, when less than 100 Americans had been killed there. And finally, the United States did not have the "God-given right to shape every nation in our own image or as we choose."

McNamara's "second thoughts" won him few friends. Vietnam veterans were outraged by his suggestion that they had been sacrificed in an unwinnable war. "McNamara should volunteer to spend a few days each month at some [Veteran's Administration] hospital," one retired air force major wrote. "Maybe then he'd see what his 'missed opportunities' cost others." The *New York Times* declared editorially that the former defense secretary's "regret cannot be huge enough to balance the books for our dead soldiers. The ghosts of those unlived lives circle close around Mr. McNamara."

soldiers to advising South Vietnam's Civilian Irregular Defense Group (CIDG). The CIDG enrolled men from the remote hill tribes of South Vietnam, such as the Montagnards who lived along the country's rugged western frontier with Cambodia and Laos, into a paramilitary (nonregular army) force. The CIDG forces specialized in small-scale backcountry operations, attacking with sudden raids and ambushes, designed to harass and spy on the Viet Cong. The Special Forces advisers lived in remote villages under primitive conditions. They shared living quarters and food with the tribesmen and often forged close relationships with them. In fact, the Montagnards—who were looked down on by other Vietnamese—felt a greater loyalty toward the Americans who armed and paid them than to the South Vietnamese government.

The Special Forces set up 18 CIDG border surveillance camps by 1964 and had nearly 20,000 CIDG fighters in arms by 1965. From the beginning, the American public developed a special affection for the soldiers of the Special Forces; they were celebrated in one magazine article as the "Harvard PhDs of warfare," and inspired the only popular song to come out of the Vietnam war, S. Sgt. Barry Sadler's 1965 hit, "Ballad of the Green Berets." Highly trained and motivated, many of the men of the Special Forces signed up for repeated tours of duty in Vietnam. But by the mid-1960s their efforts would be overshadowed by those of more conventional U.S. military units assigned to Vietnam. The army's top brass, never as enthusiastic about counterinsurgency warfare as Kennedy, were concerned that Special Forces units were draining too many experienced combat veterans away from other army units. In 1970 the last Special Forces were withdrawn from Vietnam.

American military strategy in Vietnam from 1961 to 1963 was two-pronged; while the Green Berets were out fighting an unconventional war in the bush, American advisers and equipment would be employed to help the South Vietnamese military fight a more effective conventional war against the Viet Cong. In August 1961 advisers were authorized to accompany ARVN battalions and even company-sized units on field operations. Soon afterward, American pilots began bombing raids in support of ARVN operations.

In October 1961 Kennedy sent Maxwell Taylor and Walt Rostow on a mission to assess the military situation in South Vietnam. They returned to Washington two weeks later to report to the president. Taylor urged Kennedy to provide increased logistical support for the ARVN, including air strikes and helicopters for troop transport and protection. He also called for the dispatch of 8,000 U.S. combat troops to provide security for American bases in South Vietnam. The government could send them over, saying they were needed for flood control relief; once stationed in Vietnam, they could be employed as needed in combat. Taylor dismissed the possibility that the United States might be "backing into a major Asia war" as "not impressive." But Kennedy hesitated when faced with the suggestion of sending Americans to fight in Vietnam. As he told historian and speechwriter Arthur Schlesinger, Jr.:

The troops will march in; the bands will play; the crowd will cheer; and in four days everyone will have forgotten. Then we will be told we have to send in more troops. It's like taking a drink. The effect wears off, and you have to take another.

As an alternative to Taylor's plan, Kennedy increased the number of advisers in Vietnam and stepped up logistical support. Though Kennedy was more cautious than Taylor, within two years the United States would have twice as many troops in Vietnam as Taylor had called for in his report; many of the "advisers" would be deeply involved in combat despite their title. To meet the requirements of a widening war, the American military command structure in Saigon was reorganized in February 1962 with the establishment of the U.S. Military Assistance Command, Vietnam (MACV), under the command of Gen. Paul D. Harkins.

Despite Kennedy's flat denial in a press conference in January 1962 that American troops were involved in combat in Vietnam, they were already suffering casualties. James Davis, an army specialist fourth class assigned to a research unit monitoring Viet Cong radio broadcasts, was killed in a Viet Cong ambush on December 22, 1961, the first "official" U.S. death in the Vietnam War.

Helicopter pilots and other crew members saw some of the fiercest fighting in these early days of the war. In December 1961 the first American helicopters and their crews arrived in South Vietnam and soon after began ferrying ARVN troops into battle. The helicopters provided the American command in South Vietnam with the much-prized capacity for "airmobility." Troops could be moved swiftly from distant bases to reinforce an embattled outpost or attack an enemy stronghold. The rough terrain that made up so much of Vietnam's landscape was no obstacle to them. But despite some initial successes against inexperienced Viet Cong guerrillas, helicopters did not prove to be the magic weapons that some American military strategists hoped they would.

Marine lieutenant Kenneth Babbs recalled that when he arrived in Vietnam, the U.S. military effort was still technically only an advisory one:

Our job was to haul supplies in and out of outposts; evacuate wounded; and carry ARVN on heliborne operations. We weren't supposed to participate in the fighting. But when we started taking on fire, we knew we had to be ready to protect ourselves, and we started arming our choppers . . . At first the VC were frightened by the choppers, but word must have gotten around quickly how vulnerable the machines were . . . There's so many cables and hoses running through the rotor gear box, a rifle slug could knock us out of action . . . As our tour continued, instead of running the VC stayed and fired back.

Before long, marines in Babbs's squadron were regularly involved in firefights with guerrillas on the ground. "We went in like Boy Scouts and came out like Hell's Angels," he concluded.

The Viet Cong downed their first American helicopter in February 1962. The army responded by introducing more heavily armed helicopters, like the new UH-1 gunships (nicknamed the Huey by U.S. servicemen), into Vietnam. The Hueys came armed with machine guns and rocket launchers, which could be used to suppress Viet Cong ground fire during airborne assaults. But camouflaged and dug-in guerrillas could stand up to the helicopters, as they proved in the January 2, 1963, Battle of Ap Bac. At Ap Bac, a village in the Mekong Delta, an airborne and ground ARVN assault ran into a carefully laid Viet Cong ambush. Despite the fact that the Viet Cong were outnumbered by their attackers by about 10 to one, they managed to shoot down five U.S. CH-21 ("Flying Banana") helicopters and inflict heavy casualties on the ARVN units. Sixty-one South Vietnamese soldiers were killed, and more than 100 were wounded. Three American helicopter crew members died in the battle, and 10 were wounded. Only three Viet Cong bodies were found on the battlefield. When the battle was over an American general flew to the scene to find out what had gone wrong, and was nearly killed by a badly timed artillery barrage from a "friendly" ARVN unit.

The disaster at Ap Bac provoked critical articles by some American reporters in Vietnam on ARVN's fighting abilities. Kennedy was so annoyed by negative press reports from Vietnam that he asked the publisher of the *New York Times* to reassign its correspondent David Halberstam elsewhere (the *Times* refused). Farther from the field, it was easy to take comfort in optimistic reports that poured out from ARVN and MACV headquarters. Robert McNamara, secretary of defense, on his return from his first visit to South Vietnam in 1962, declared: "Every quantitative measurement we have shows we're winning the war." A South Vietnamese general once explained to an American official why the Americans' preoccupation with *"les statistiques"* amused their allies:

Tight formation of U.S. Army CH-21 ("Flying Banana") helicopters
supports South Vietnamese attacks on Viet Cong jungle bases north
of Saigon. Machine guns are manned in the helicopter doors.
(National Archives)

"We Vietnamese can give [McNamara] all he wants. If you want them to
go up, they will go up. If you want them to go down, they will go down."

The South Vietnamese were not the only military officers capable of
statistical inflation. On the basis of briefings they received from MACV
commander Paul Harkins, Robert McNamara and Maxwell Taylor
returned from a visit to Saigon in September 1963 and in a report to the
president on October 2 declared the military campaign had made such
"great progress" that 1,000 U.S. troops could be withdrawn by the end
of the year, and sufficient progress could be achieved by 1965 so that "it
should be possible to withdraw the bulk of U.S. personnel at that time."

On a visit to Saigon in May 1961, Vice President Lyndon Johnson
had called South Vietnamese president Diem "the Churchill of Asia." In
reality, U.S. officials were increasingly concerned about Diem's capabilities as a leader. Diem ignored repeated requests from Washington to
introduce reforms that would make his government more popular and
his army more efficient. Diem felt he could count on American support
regardless of his policies.

Ngo Dinh Nhu, Diem's younger brother, headed the South Vietnamese secret police and helped Diem crush protest against his regime with a heavy hand. Among the various noncommunist groups who resented Diem's rule were the many South Vietnamese who were followers of the Buddhist religion. They had long resented the Catholic minority that dominated the government. At Nhu's urging, Diem adopted a harsh line toward the Buddhist protests that rocked South Vietnam in the spring and summer of 1963. On May 8, 1963, nine Buddhists (seven of them children) were killed in the city of Hue by government troops for defying an official ban on displaying the Buddhist flag during their celebration of Buddha's birthday. On June 11, 1963, an aged Buddhist monk named Quang Duc had himself doused with gasoline, then lit a match and burned to death to protest religious discrimination in South Vietnam. Photos of his flaming body were reprinted in newspapers around the world and did much to discredit Diem's government. So, too, did a comment by Diem's sister-in-law, Madame Ngo Dinh Nhu (dubbed the "Dragon Lady" by American reporters), who called the monk's suicide a "barbecue" and offered to buy matches and gasoline for anyone else planning a similar protest. Quang Duc's martyrdom spurred mass demonstrations in the streets of South Vietnam's cities. Six more Buddhists burned themselves to death that summer of 1963. U.S. ambassador to Saigon Frederick Nolting tried to persuade Diem to make concessions to the Buddhists, but in late August American-trained units of the government special forces raided Buddhist pagodas across South Vietnam, arresting 1,400 monks and vandalizing shrines. The United States publicly denounced the raids, blaming Diem's brother Nhu for them and demanding his ouster from the government.

When Diem refused to dump Nhu, a key group of Kennedy advisers (including Henry Cabot Lodge, Nolting's replacement as ambassador to Saigon) turned against him. They responded favorably when approached by a group of South Vietnamese generals in late August who proposed to overthrow Diem in a military coup. Lodge cabled Secretary of State Dean Rusk on August 29, declaring, "We are launched on a course from which there is no respectable turning back: the overthrow of the Diem government." The generals drew back from the coup attempt at the last moment, but U.S. officials hoped they would try again. The White House cabled Lodge on October 6 that though it did not wish to "stimulate" a coup, it also did not want "to leave the impression that the U.S. would thwart a change in government." Washington's chief concern was over the public relations aspects of the affair. McGeorge Bundy, national security adviser, cabled Ambassador Lodge on October 25: "We are particularly concerned about [the] hazard that an unsuccessful coup, however carefully we avoid direct engagement, will be laid at our door by public opinion."

Finally convinced that they had U.S. backing, the generals made their move on November 1, 1963, seizing key military installations in Saigon. While the battle was still raging outside the presidential palace in Saigon, Diem telephoned Ambassador Lodge, who pretended to know nothing about what was going on. Diem and Nhu fled the presidential palace, but were captured in the Catholic church where they had sought refuge. Their captors shot and stabbed them to death in the back of an armored personnel carrier, something that the leaders in Washington who encouraged the coup had not counted on.

When Kennedy learned of Diem's murder, he turned pale and fled the room without a word. Three days later, notwithstanding the murders, the United States recognized the new provisional government in Saigon. Three weeks later John F. Kennedy was assassinated in Dallas. When Kennedy had taken office in January 1961, the United States had about 900 servicemen stationed in Vietnam. When he died in November 1963 that number had increased to more than 16,000. One hundred and twenty Americans had already died in Vietnam. It was now up to the new president, Lyndon Baines Johnson, to determine how—and how long—to carry on in Vietnam.

5

JOHNSON'S WAR

——✦—⊷⊶⊷——————————————————

1963–1964

The Vietnam War differed from other American wars in which there were clearly defined dividing lines between peace and war: the firing on Fort Sumter that marked the start of the Civil War, for instance, or the Japanese attack on Pearl Harbor that marked the start of World War II in the Pacific. Most American wars began with the formal declaration of war by Congress required by the U.S. Constitution. The Korean War was the first major foreign war that the United States fought without a congressional declaration of war; U.S. soldiers fought in that conflict under the banner of the United Nations, their presence authorized by vote of the U.N. Security Council.

In the case of the war in Vietnam, there was no congressional declaration of war, and no single event or decision clearly marked its beginning. Arguments can be made to date the "start" of the war from the Eisenhower years, the Kennedy years, or the Johnson years. What can be said without qualification is that in the first years of Johnson's presidency, a point of no return was reached in the Vietnam conflict. Secret decisions made in Washington in 1964 committed the United States to step up drastically the level of its military involvement in the war in Vietnam.

When Lyndon Johnson became president in November 1963, he sought to prove to the nation that he would carry out Kennedy's legacy in both domestic and international policy. That meant there could be no talk of withdrawal from Vietnam. Three days after Kennedy's assassination, Johnson issued a national security memo-

On November 24, 1963, one day after Kennedy's assassination, President Johnson confers with members of the executive staff: (from left) U.S. Ambassador to Vietnam Henry Cabot Lodge; Secretary of State Dean Rusk; the president; Secretary of Defense Robert McNamara; and Undersecretary of State George W. Ball. *(National Archives)*

randum declaring that he expected "all senior officers of the government" to provide "full unity of support for established U.S. policy in South Vietnam."

Washington policy makers would soon conclude, however, that the "established U.S. policy" had proven a failure. When Defense Secretary Robert McNamara returned from a visit to Vietnam in December 1963, he again assured the public that great progress was being made in the war. Privately, however, he warned the president that "current trends" in the war in Vietnam "will lead to neutralization at best or more likely to a Communist-controlled state." Returning to Saigon in March 1964, McNamara reported to Johnson that things had "unquestionably been growing worse" since his last visit. The Communists were extending their control over more and more of the countryside and the new South Vietnamese government was proving even more ineffective than the Diem regime overthrown the previous fall.

In Saigon, the military council headed by Duong Van Minh (nicknamed "Big Minh" by the Americans) was overthrown in January 1964 by a group of younger officers led by Gen. Nguyen Khanh, commander of the ARVN First Corps. But Khanh himself had only the shakiest grip on power. There would be a total of three coups and five new governments in power in Saigon between November 1963 and February 1965. American leaders despaired of ever finding a viable successor to Diem. "I don't think we ought to take this government seriously," Ambassador Henry Cabot Lodge complained to Johnson in the summer of 1965. "There is simply no one who can do anything." After a series of short-lived military governments, Gen. Nguyen Van Thieu and Air Vice Marshal Nguyen Cao Ky emerged as South Vietnam's strongmen. Thieu and Ky's triumph provided a measure of stability in Saigon, if not of greatly increased efficiency or popularity for the government. Ky was a swashbuckling figure, well known for his costume of dark sunglasses, fancy-cut silk fatigue uniforms, and silk scarf wound around his neck. He carried a pearl-handled revolver in his holster. "At least no one can mistake him for Ho Chi Minh," a U.S. general once remarked about Ky's

President Johnson is introduced to South Vietnam's prime minister, Nguyen Cao Ky; Secretary of State Dean Rusk shakes hands with Vietnamese chief of state Nguyen Van Thieu. At left are Madame Ky and Chief of Protocol Lloyd Hand, February 6, 1966. *(National Archives)*

taste in clothing. Thieu, more cautious and conservative, eventually maneuvered Ky out of power. He would use the office of president of South Vietnam to enrich himself and his supporters.

Meanwhile the Communists continued to increase their strength in the south. The Viet Cong grew to a force of an estimated 170,000 soldiers in 1964. Most of their recruits still came from the south, but Hanoi also stepped up infiltration in 1964, sending regular North Vietnamese troops to fight alongside the southerners. The Ho Chi Minh trail, little more than a series of footpaths in the late 1950s, had by now been equipped with bridges, hospitals, antiaircraft defenses, barracks, and warehouses along its length. The Viet Cong, who at first had made do with outmoded weapons left over from the war with the French, now carried increasingly sophisticated weapons, including Soviet and Chinese-manufactured AK-47 automatic assault rifles—weapons that many American soldiers considered superior to their own M-16 rifles.

In the cities, the Viet Cong made their presence felt through frequent bomb attacks. In Saigon in February 1964 two Americans were killed in a movie theater bombing. In the countryside the strategic hamlet program, the main prop of the government's "pacification" campaign, was left near collapse through a combination of Viet Cong attacks and peasant dissatisfaction. And in the military struggle between the Viet Cong and the ARVN, the Viet Cong inflicted heavy losses on their opponents.

July 1964 was a month of especially fierce fighting. Sometimes it involved Americans. Shortly after 2 A.M. on July 6, a 500-man Viet Cong unit attacked the Nam Dong Special Forces camp near South Vietnam's border with Laos. The camp was guarded by 12 American Green Berets and several hundred Vietnamese Civil Guards. After a mortar barrage, the attackers broke through the barbed wire of the camp's outer defense lines. The South Vietnamese and American defenders had to use their artillery at point-blank range to beat back the Viet Cong. Special Forces captain Roger Donlon rallied the camp's defenders. Under heavy fire, he killed three Viet Cong commandos as they attempted to destroy the main gate. Though wounded in the stomach, shoulder, and leg, Donlon crawled across the camp dragging a heavy ammunition load to one of his mortar positions, where he directed the fire against the attackers. When dawn came, the Viet Cong withdrew, leaving 60 of their dead behind, but 58 South Vietnamese soldiers and two Americans had also been killed. Donlon himself survived and was awarded the Medal of Honor, the first of 239 American servicemen in Vietnam who would win the nation's highest military award.

In other battles that month the South Vietnamese suffered a string of defeats. An ARVN outpost at Chuong Thien was attacked on July 11–12 and a relief force coming to its aid was ambushed, with 200 ARVN casualties. The following day an ARVN convoy was ambushed 40 miles south of Saigon, with 16 ARVN soldiers and three Americans killed. On July 26 another ARVN convoy was ambushed in Chuong Thien Province, with more than 100 ARVN casualties.

With the war apparently being lost on the ground in South Vietnam, American military and political leaders concluded that the solution to their problems lay in expanding it to the air over North Vietnam. "We are swatting flies," U.S. Air Force Chief of Staff Curtis LeMay declared in December 1963, "when we should be going after the manure pile." Walt Rostow, chairman of the State Department's Policy Planning Staff, argued in a February memorandum to Secretary of State Dean Rusk that Communists in North Vietnam were more vulnerable to American military pressure than Communists fighting in South Vietnam. Ho Chi Minh "has an industrial complex to protect: he is no longer a guerrilla fighter with nothing to lose." At the same time, Rostow proposed that the president consider approaching Congress for a resolution backing American military actions in Vietnam as a substitute for a formal declaration of war.

In April 1964 the Joint Chiefs of Staff drew up a list of 94 potential targets for bombing in North Vietnam. In May William Bundy, who had moved from the Defense Department to the State Department earlier in the year, drew up a scenario for a 30-day program of military escalation leading to full-scale bombing attacks against North Vietnam. He also drew up a draft of a resolution for Congress along the lines that Rostow had earlier proposed. President Johnson was sympathetic to his advisers' calls for expanding the war, but postponed acting on them until after the November 1964 U.S. presidential election.

Johnson was less restrained in expanding America's "secret war" in Southeast Asia. Since 1961 the United States had been waging war in Laos against the Pathet Lao and the North Vietnamese operating along the Ho Chi Minh trail, with an army of Mco tribesmen who were equipped, paid, and advised by the CIA. Johnson now authorized an air war to support the CIA's ground war in Laos. American and Thai pilots, flying planes provided by Air America, a CIA-run airline, flew bombing missions over Laos. And in February 1964, the United States launched a campaign of covert attacks on North Vietnam, known by its code name, Operation Plan 34-A (OPlan 34-A). Teams of South Vietnamese commandos were parachuted into North Vietnam, where they attempted without much success, to blow up rail and highway bridges. South Vietnamese PT boats bombarded North Vietnamese coastal installations. American destroyers carrying sophisticated electronic receiving devices were sent on patrol off the coast of North Vietnam. These DeSoto patrols, as they were code-named, were intended to apply psychological pressure and to gather information about North Vietnamese coastal defenses. The existence of the 34A operations was kept a closely guarded secret from the American public.

While key decisions were being made in Washington, the American leadership in Saigon also underwent some changes. In June, Johnson appointed Maxwell Taylor to succeed Henry Cabot Lodge as American ambassador to South Vietnam. (Lodge would return for a second tour as ambassador in 1965.) Taylor had been an early advocate of an expanded American military presence in South Vietnam, calling for the introduction of U.S. combat troops in 1961. Gen. William Westmoreland replaced Paul Harkins as commander of the U.S. Military Assistance Command, Vietnam (MACV). Westmoreland ("Westy" to his friends) was a much decorated veteran of World War II and the Korean War, who had been serving as superintendent of the U.S. Military Academy at West Point when he was assigned to be Harkins's deputy in Vietnam in 1963. Harkins had fallen out of favor in Washington the previous fall, when he opposed the plotting that led to the overthrow of Diem. As Harkins's successor, Westmoreland was destined to oversee the great expansion of the American military effort in Vietnam between 1964 and 1968.

Johnson had always been a firm believer in the domino theory, declaring upon his return from a 1961 vice presidential trip to South Vietnam that if the United States did not defeat Communists in that country, it would wind up fighting them "on the beaches of Waikiki." In the spring of 1965 he asked the CIA to decide if the theory was really true: "Would the rest of Southeast Asia necessarily fall if Laos and South Vietnam came under North Vietnamese control?" The CIA replied on June 9 that "with the possible exception of Cambodia, it is likely that no nation in the area would quickly succumb to Communism as a result of the fall of Laos and South Vietnam," which turned out to be a very accurate prediction.

But Johnson and his advisers ignored the CIA's answer. They believed that North Vietnam was merely a puppet of Communist China, and that China, like Hitler's Germany in the 1930s and Stalin's Soviet Union in the 1940s, would not stop attacking or subverting its neighbors unless its aggressive tendencies were contained by outside force, such as the United States was applying in South Vietnam. And it was not just China's neighbors that were in danger. The Soviet Union would also be watching how the United States conducted itself in Vietnam; an American failure would encourage the Soviets to renew their own expansionist drive. Secretary of State Dean Rusk declared in July 1964 that if the United States let South Vietnam fall to the Communists, then "our guarantees with regard to Berlin would lose their credibility." A year later LBJ would declare: "If we are driven from the field in Vietnam, then no nation can ever again have the same confidence in American protection." Perhaps the clearest description of American goals in South Vietnam was offered, secretly, in a memorandum from John McNaughton, assistant secretary of defense, to Robert McNamara in March 1965. "U.S. Aims" in South Vietnam were:

> 70%—To avoid a humiliating U.S. defeat (to our reputation as guarantor).
> 20%—To keep SVN (and the adjacent) territory from Chinese hands.
> 10%—To permit the people of SVN to enjoy a better, freer way of life.

Maintaining U.S. credibility would remain a primary concern for American policy makers at every stage of the Vietnam war.

The only doubts Johnson developed about American policies in Vietnam had more to do with domestic than international concerns. Johnson had taken office at a time of great social change. The civil rights movement led by Dr. Martin Luther King, Jr., was challenging racial discrimination in the South. The movement had helped unleash a wave of optimism and idealism in the nation. Johnson rode that wave in gaining congressional passage of important civil rights legislation. He also asked Congress to fund a "war on poverty"—which, he hoped, would make it possible for all Americans to enjoy a decent standard of living in what he called the "Great Society." A major war in Vietnam could only damage his hopes for domestic reform, as he told an interviewer years later:

Dr. Martin Luther King, Jr., in a crowd at the civil rights march on Washington, D.C., August 28, 1963. *(National Archives)*

I knew from the start that I was bound to be crucified either way I moved. If I left the woman I really loved—the Great Society—in order to get involved with that bitch of a war on the other side of the world, then I would lose everything at home. All my programs. All my hopes to feed the hungry and shelter the homeless. All my dreams to provide education and medical care to the browns and the blacks and the lame and the poor. But if I left that war and let the Communists take over South Vietnam, then I would be seen as a coward and my nation would be seen as an appeaser, and we would both find it impossible to accomplish anything for anybody anywhere on the entire globe.

Already in the spring of 1964, as that year's presidential campaign heated up, Johnson was under attack from Republican politicians for not doing enough in Vietnam to defeat the Communists. Barry Goldwater, the leading candidate for the Republican nomination for the presidency, proposed in a speech in May 1964 that the United States use atomic bombs in South Vietnam to "defoliate" the forests where the Viet Cong were based, and bomb the transportation links that connected North Vietnam with China. Later that summer, Goldwater secured the Republican nomination. But before the summer was over, events had taken place in Vietnam that defused the Republican challenge to Johnson's Vietnam policies.

On July 30, the U.S. destroyer *Maddox* entered the Gulf of Tonkin, the coastal waters that lie alongside North Vietnam. The *Maddox* was on a DeSoto patrol, electronically gathering information about North Vietnamese defense capabilities. OPlan 34-A was in full swing. That same day, South Vietnamese commandos raided the North Vietnamese islands of Hon Me and Hon Nieu in the Gulf of Tonkin. And on August 1 and 2, Thai pilots flying U.S. planes bombed North Vietnamese villages near the Laotian border. The North Vietnamese were on edge, expecting further assaults at any moment. In the next few days the *Maddox* sailed as close as eight miles to the North Vietnamese mainland and four miles to the two islands raided by the South Vietnamese commandos.

On the night of August 2, three North Vietnamese torpedo boats sailed at high speed toward the *Maddox* (possibly believing that it was a South Vietnamese vessel involved in the July 30 raid). In the 37-minute sea battle that followed, two of the torpedo boats were damaged by American planes based on a nearby aircraft carrier, the USS *Ticon-*

deroga, and a third was knocked out of commission by shell fire from the *Maddox*'s five-inch guns. The North Vietnamese ships managed to fire three torpedoes before being driven off, but none did any damage. There were no U.S. casualties in the encounter.

The U.S. Navy ordered another destroyer, the *C. Turner Joy,* to join the *Maddox* in the Gulf of Tonkin. The next night, August 3, South Vietnamese torpedo boats raided the North Vietnamese coast. From intercepted North Vietnamese radio traffic, the United States knew that the North Vietnamese believed there was a connection between the destroyers' patrols and the raids. The crew of the destroyers expected a new North Vietnamese attack at any moment.

On the evening of August 4, sailors aboard the two U.S. destroyers began to pick up radar and sonar readings indicating the presence of enemy ships. The alarm was sounded. Although there were no visual sightings of enemy ships, several sailors claimed to have seen torpedo wakes heading toward the destroyers. Over the next two hours, seamen manning sonar equipment reported 26 torpedoes fired at the *Maddox.* The *Maddox* and the *Turner Joy* fired 400 shells in the direction they thought the attack was coming from.

They also called in air support from the USS *Ticonderoga.* Navy pilot James Stockdale flew to the scene of the battle in his F-8E Crusader fighter, prepared to sink the enemy ships. For an hour and a half, sometimes flying so low that his plane was splashed by the ocean, he crisscrossed the area looking for the enemy. He later reported that there was "not a ship, not the outline of a ship, not a wake" where the North Vietnamese torpedo boats were supposed to have been. "Not a reflection, not the light of a single tracer bullet. Nothing."

The captain of the *Maddox,* John Herrick, finally called off the engagement, cabling his superiors: "Entire action leaves many doubts. Suggest complete evaluation before any further action." Later it would be suggested that an inexperienced and jittery sonar man aboard the *Maddox* had mistaken the sound of his own ship's rudder for onrushing enemy torpedoes, while freak weather conditions led to misinterpretation of radar readings. It seems likely that there were no North Vietnamese ships in the area that night.

But Lyndon Johnson, back in Washington, D.C., did not wait to find out what exactly happened that night in the Gulf of Tonkin. He cast aside his remaining hesitations about striking hard and directly at the North Vietnamese. News of the incident in the Tonkin Gulf reached

Washington in the late morning of August 4 (there is a 12-hour time difference between Vietnam and the U.S. East Coast). Contingency plans for attacking North Vietnam, which had been drawn up in the spring, were put into effect. During the day Johnson met with congressional leaders to inform them of his plans. Then, just before midnight of August 4, he went on television to speak to the public. American ships, he announced, had been attacked on the high seas. In retaliation, U.S. aircraft were already on their way to bomb North Vietnam. He ended with the pledge, "We still seek no wider war." After Johnson's announcement, however, McNamara went before the cameras to provide a detailed account of the "sea battle," including the claim that at least two North Vietnamese Navy (NVN) ships had been sunk in the attack.

On board the *Ticonderoga,* Commander Stockdale was assigned to lead a reprisal attack against the North Vietnamese fuel depot at Vinh City. When told of his mission, his first reaction was "Reprisal for what?" Planes from the aircraft carriers *Ticonderoga* and *Constellation* flew 64 sorties against NVN facilities, destroying the Vinh City depot, PT boat bases, and antiaircraft installations. Two U.S. planes were shot down. Lt. (jg) Rather Sather was killed, the first American pilot to die over North Vietnam; the other pilot, Lt. (jg) Everett Alvarez, was taken prisoner by the North Vietnamese. As he approached his assigned target in his A-4 Skyhawk, Alvarez recalled:

> We made an identification pass, then came around and made an actual pass, firing. I was very low, just skimming the trees at about five hundred knots. Then I had the weirdest feeling. My airplane was hit and started to fall apart, rolling and burning. I knew I would not live if I stayed with the airplane, so I ejected, and luckily I cleared a cliff.

Alvarez fractured his back in the drop. He would be held captive until 1973. Stockdale would be shot down over North Vietnam in 1965 and captured. He also remained a prisoner until 1973, the highest-ranking U.S. Navy prisoner of war.

Privately Johnson was skeptical about the August 4 incident, remarking to an aide, "Hell, those dumb stupid sailors were just shooting at flying fish." But following the script devised by his advisers that spring, he took the opportunity to go before Congress to ask for a resolution authorizing him to "take all necessary measures to repel an

Lyndon Johnson as 1964's "Peace Candidate"

OF ALL THE POLITICAL ADVANTAGES THAT LYNDON Johnson enjoyed in the 1964 presidential race, perhaps most important was the masterful job he had done in reassuring and uniting a grieving nation in the aftermath of John F. Kennedy's assassination. In his first televised presidential address, delivered less than a week after Kennedy's death in November 1963, he quoted the slain president's words from his 1961 inaugural address: "Let us begin." Johnson now added his own pledge: "Let us continue." And he proceeded to make good on that promise, pushing Congress to enact landmark civil rights and antipoverty legislation as a tribute to the late president.

But there was one dark cloud on the electoral horizon, and that was the Vietnam War. Here, the "Kennedy legacy" proved a burden. Americans were already debating what Kennedy would have done in Vietnam, had he lived—a debate that would continue among historians, journalists, and others for decades afterward. Doing too little in Vietnam would leave Johnson vulnerable to charges from conservatives that he was betraying the Kennedy legacy of resolute cold war leadership by allowing the country to fall to the Communists. Doing too much in Vietnam would leave him equally vulnerable to charges from liberals that he was betraying Kennedy's legacy of limited commitments in the region, leading the United States into a dangerous, open-ended conflict in Southeast Asia.

That is why the Gulf of Tonkin incident proved to be a political godsend. Four months before the November presidential election, Johnson hit back at the Communists for allegedly attacking U.S. warships—but his retaliation was limited to a one-time air strike. He thus established his political credentials with American voters as both commander in chief and as a "man of peace." Barry Goldwater had no chance against that potent combination.

armed attack against the forces of the United States and to prevent further aggression." This measure became known as the Tonkin Gulf Resolution and served as the legal justification for the war until its repeal in 1970. The resolution passed the House of Representatives unanimously and passed with only two dissenting votes in the Senate, those of Ernest Gruening of Alaska and Wayne Morse of Oregon.

Morse called the legislation a "predated resolution of war," and predicted that many who voted for it would later come to regret their choice. OPlan 34-A remained a secret. Robert McNamara went before a Senate committee on August 6 to give testimony in support of the Tonkin Gulf Resolution, and denied that the *Maddox* and *Turner Joy* were involved in anything more than a routine patrol in international waters.

According to public opinion polls, 85 percent of the public approved of the raids against North Vietnam. Johnson's personal popularity in the polls skyrocketed. He had proven that he was willing to stand up to the Communists; now he was free to turn around and portray his opponent, Barry Goldwater, as an irresponsible warmonger. At a campaign rally at his Texas ranch on August 29, Johnson declared:

> I have had advice to load our planes with bombs and to drop them on certain areas that I think would enlarge the war and escalate the war, and result in our committing a good many American boys to fighting a war that I think ought to be fought by the boys of Asia to help protect their own land.

On November 3, 1964, Johnson was reelected in a landslide victory, with 61 percent of the popular vote. But Johnson, the peace candidate in 1964, was about to approve plans to lead his nation into a much wider war.

6

ON THE
TIGER'S BACK

———◆◈◈◈———

1964–1965

In the aftermath of the Gulf of Tonkin incident, American political and military leaders secretly committed the United States to fighting an expanded war in Indochina. Their plans included a systematic bombing campaign against North Vietnam. In mid-August 1964, William Bundy outlined a plan for a gradual escalation of the war to culminate in bombing early in 1965. This was the same man who the previous May had drawn up the draft of what became the Tonkin Gulf Resolution. In early September John McNaughton, assistant secretary of defense, sent a memorandum to Defense Secretary Robert McNamara suggesting yet another scenario. This involved provocative actions that could be taken against North Vietnam, including South Vietnamese air strikes on the Ho Chi Minh trail in Laos and seaborne raids on the North Vietnamese coast. Assuming that the North Vietnamese responded with new attacks of their own, McNaughton's plan would "provide good grounds for us to escalate if we wish" with a bombing campaign. On September 7, a White House strategy meeting of Johnson's top advisers agreed that the war would be carried to North Vietnam once the U.S. presidential election was over.

Johnson's military and political advisers agreed on the need to expand the war, but disagreed over the scale and timing of escalation. The military wanted to launch an immediate and full-scale bombing offensive, while the civilians wanted a step-by-step program of escalation.

The air force chief of staff, Gen. Curtis LeMay, argued that U.S. strategy should be to bomb North Vietnam "back to the Stone Age." Civilian policy makers argued that a graduated approach to escalation, a sort of slow squeeze, would allow the United States to test Ho Chi Minh's resolve without risking expanding the war to China or the Soviet Union. Sooner or later, these civilians argued, the U.S. military attacks would reach the "threshold" of pain and suffering that North Vietnamese leaders would no longer find acceptable to obtain their goals in South Vietnam. On the other hand, some civilian advisers, among them Walt Rostow, were already advocating the dispatch of U.S. combat troops to South Vietnam, a step that the military's Joint Chiefs of Staff were still reluctant to consider in the fall of 1964.

As far as direct attacks on North Vietnam were concerned, Johnson leaned toward the more cautious approach favored by his civilian advisers. American fighter-bombers in the Pacific remained on their carrier

Gen. Curtis LeMay advocated extensive bombing of North Vietnam in 1964.
(Library of Congress, Prints and Photographs Division [LC-USZ62-90918])

decks for the moment, but Johnson did authorize the resumption of DeSoto patrols in the Gulf of Tonkin in September 1964 and South Vietnamese coastal raids on North Vietnam that October.

The one dissenter from the pro-escalation consensus in Johnson's inner circle of advisers was his undersecretary of state, George Ball, who had earlier tried to convince Kennedy to reconsider American policy in South Vietnam. Disturbed by the steps being considered to expand the war, Ball drafted a long memorandum in October 1964 that challenged the basic assumptions of current American policy. The solution in Vietnam, Ball argued, should be pursued by political and diplomatic rather than military means. American international credibility would suffer more from irresponsible escalation of the war than from possible Communist gains in Southeast Asia: "What we might gain by establishing the steadfastness of our commitments," through escalation, "we could lose by an erosion of confidence in our judgments."

Ball worried that even a graduated policy of escalation could get out of hand. If the United States upped the ante of violence in Vietnam, the Communists might well respond with increasing their own commitment, which would require a still greater American commitment, and on and on with no end in sight. "Once on the tiger's back," he warned prophetically, "we cannot be sure of picking the place to dismount." Johnson did not get around to reading Ball's memorandum until February 1965. He paid little attention to it even then, although he respected the role that Ball was playing as "devil's advocate" within an administration where few shared his concerns.

Johnson had no intention of revealing any dramatic changes in American policy in Vietnam until after he was safely elected to the White House in November. He made that clear on November 1, two days before the presidential election, when a Viet Cong mortar barrage on the Bien Hoa airfield in South Vietnam killed five Americans and destroyed six B-57 bombers. Johnson turned down a request by the Joint Chiefs of Staff for reprisal air raids against North Vietnam. That same day, however, he appointed a committee headed by Assistant Secretary of State William Bundy to study future U.S. military options in Vietnam. Bundy came back to the president three weeks later presenting the choices, as his committee saw them: the United States could continue more or less on its present course, perhaps launching more reprisal bombing attacks against North Vietnam; the United States could immediately launch an all-out bombing campaign against North Vietnam; or the United States could launch a graduated series of attacks, first against the Ho Chi Minh trail in Laos and then moving on to North Vietnam. The options of lowering the level of violence, offering negotiations, or withdrawing were not considered by Bundy and his committee.

Like most of his advisers, Johnson favored the last of Bundy's options, which seemed to him to represent the moderate path between

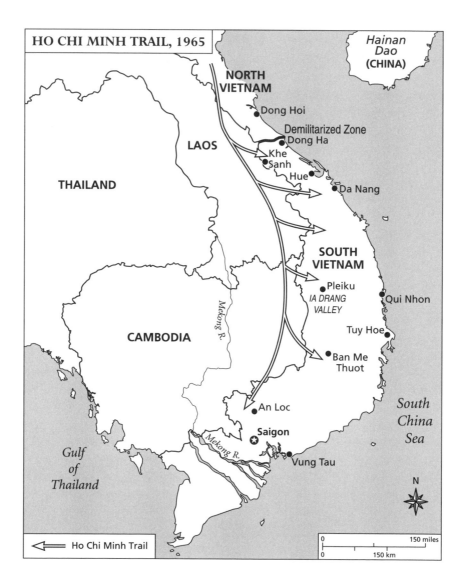

At 5:55 P.M. on December 24, 1964, Viet Cong terrorists exploded a bomb in front of the Brinks Hotel in Saigon, South Vietnam. *(National Archives)*

the two extremes of light bombing or all-out bombing. At secret meetings in the White House in early December, the reelected president gave final approval to the plan for air strikes to be launched against the north as soon as an appropriate incident provided justification for U.S. reprisal. This would be followed by a sustained bombing campaign. The first step in the plan was launched shortly afterward when the United States secretly began air strikes in Laos.

Though Johnson was by now safely elected and had given his approval to his advisers' plan for the air war against North Vietnam, he stalled on giving the order to launch the bombers. He could not shake nagging doubts as to the effectiveness of the whole strategy. On Christmas Eve, the Viet Cong presented him with the perfect pretext for retaliatory air attacks when they exploded a car bomb in front of the Brinks Hotel in Saigon, which was being used to house American officers. Two Americans were killed in the attack and dozens were wounded. Maxwell

Taylor, the American ambassador in Saigon, and General Westmoreland, the MACV commander, immediately asked Johnson to launch raids on North Vietnam. Yet Johnson refused.

In a cable to Taylor the president complained, "Every time I get a military recommendation, it seems to me that it calls for a large-scale bombing." He still did not believe that the war could be won from the air. That did not mean that Johnson opposed escalating the war. Instead, he was thinking about "a larger and stronger use of rangers and special forces and marines" on the ground in South Vietnam. He made it clear in his cable that if Taylor or General Westmoreland called for the commitment of ground forces, their request would "have immediate attention from me." When he sent this cable at the end of 1964, the United States had 23,000 military personnel in South Vietnam, an increase of 7,000 since Kennedy's death, all of them still designated as "advisers." The United States had lost 267 men killed in action in South Vietnam since 1961, 147 of them in 1964.

Despite Johnson's misgivings, the momentum for air war could not be stopped. On January 14, 1965, Ambassador Taylor received another cable from the White House. This one ordered that "immediately following the occurrence of a spectacular enemy action" he should "propose to us what reprisal action you considered desirable." The necessary "spectacular enemy action" came along three weeks later at Pleiku, the site of a U.S. airbase in the Central Highlands of South Vietnam, its airstrip crowded with transport and observation aircraft and helicopters. At 2 A.M. on February 7, 1965, the airstrip and a barracks a few miles away were hit simultaneously by a Viet Cong mortar and ground attack. In 15 minutes, eight Americans were killed, more than 100 were wounded, and 10 U.S. aircraft were destroyed.

Johnson's National Security Advisor, McGeorge Bundy, happened to be in Saigon on the last day of a fact-finding mission when he received news of the attack. Following a meeting with General Westmoreland and Ambassador Taylor, Bundy telephoned Johnson in Washington and urged that the United States launch its long-delayed reprisal strikes. Johnson called together his national security council for a meeting, and announced, "I have had enough of this."

Within hours Operation Flaming Dart was launched, as fighter-bombers from the carriers *Ranger, Coral Sea,* and *Hancock* attacked a guerrilla training camp in North Vietnam. More attacks followed in the next few days from land- and carrier-based U.S. and South Vietnamese planes. On February 13, Johnson authorized the start of Operation Rolling Thunder, the sustained bombing campaign against North Vietnam. Rolling Thunder was temporarily delayed because of a coup attempt in Saigon, but began in earnest on March 2, 1965. Before the month was out, shipments of Soviet "SAM" surface-to-air missiles began to arrive in the North Vietnamese port of Haiphong. Although no one knew it at the time, Operation Rolling Thunder was destined to last, with only minor interruptions, for the next three and a half years. By the time Rolling Thunder ended in October 1968, the United States had dropped 643,000 tons of bombs on North Vietnam, at a cost of 922 aircraft shot down over the country.

When news of the first bombing raid was announced in the United States, the polls showed a surge of public support for the president. Most Americans believed that bombing North Vietnam was justified by the attack on Pleiku. McGeorge Bundy revealed perhaps more than he intended about the real meaning of Pleiku when he spoke to a reporter a few days after the start of Operation Flaming Dart. The reporter asked what was so different between the attack on Pleiku and the earlier attacks on Americans at the Brinks Hotel and Bien Hoa airfield, which had not called forth any U.S. military reprisals against the north. "Pleikus are like streetcars," Bundy replied, which was to say they came along regularly and you could climb on whichever one was most convenient.

In fact, every time the president took decisive military action abroad, his popularity surged upward. The polls reinforced Johnson's belief that he was doing the right thing in Vietnam. What he would discover in time was that the polls were misleading. Although each act of escalation made Johnson more popular for a few days or weeks, in the months and years to come the overall impact of these decisions would undermine the public's confidence in his administration. Too many decisions were being made behind closed doors and sprung on the American people. As early as the spring of 1965 the press began to speak of a "credibility gap" existing between the Johnson administration's words and deeds.

The next fateful step in the war's escalation came in early March 1965. In February General Westmoreland had cabled Washington asking for the dispatch of two battalions of U.S. Marines to protect the American airbase at Da Nang. Johnson agreed. Only as an afterthought was the South Vietnamese government informed of the American decision to transform the nature of the war being fought on its territory and in its name. On February 26 the State Department cabled to Ambassador Taylor: "Approved deployment [of Marines]. Secure GVN [South Vietnam's government] approval." At 9:03 A.M. on March 8 U.S. Marines in full combat gear began wading ashore on the beaches of Da Nang. The scene resembled the World War II landings on Japanese-held islands in the Pacific. This time, however, the marines were not greeted by a hail of artillery and machine gun fire. Instead they were met by a delegation of young Vietnamese women distributing flower garlands and by four U.S. Army advisers who poked fun at their rivals' dramatic arrival with a handpainted banner reading "Welcome to the gallant Marines."

By March 12, 3,500 marines were ashore. The Pentagon's press release on March 6 announcing the decision to send them referred to the "limited mission" the marines would be expected to perform in South Vietnam. They would simply be relieving government forces "now engaged in security duties for action . . . in offensive roles against Communist guerrilla forces." There was no pretense that the new American troops were "advisers" like the thousands who had preceded them, but there was the suggestion that American boys would not be doing any serious fighting in South Vietnam. They were there to do guard duty; it

A landing craft brings marines and their heavy equipment ashore at Da Nang, March 8, 1965. (U.S. Marine Corps)

was ARVN, the South Vietnamese army, that would still do the fighting in the jungles and rice paddies.

But once the prohibition against sending ground combat forces into South Vietnam was broken, it proved impossible for policy makers to hold the line on either their numbers or their mission. On March 13 General Westmoreland drew up a report on the situation in South Vietnam, which ended with a call for the commitment of 40,000 more troops. By mid-April American officials meeting in Honolulu agreed to increase the U.S. troop level to more than 80,000. By the end of July, Johnson publicly announced that the troop level would be increased to 125,000. By the end of the year the actual number of U.S. troops in South Vietnam had grown to more than 180,000.

In their first few weeks "in country," the marines were restricted to guarding three coastal enclaves around the U.S. bases at Da Nang, Phu Bai, and Chu Lai. This was the strategy favored by Ambassador Taylor. But General Westmoreland wanted the authority to order American fighting men into combat anywhere in South Vietnam that they were needed. In early April a new policy governing the use of American troops was adopted, representing a compromise between Taylor's and Westmoreland's positions. U.S. forces could now patrol up to 50 miles from their enclaves, instead of just sitting in defensive positions and waiting for the enemy to come to them.

The U.S. Marines were soon only part of a much larger combat force newly deployed in Vietnam. Soldiers from the 173rd Airborne Brigade arrived in South Vietnam in May, the first U.S. Army combat unit in the country. The famed 101st ("Screaming Eagles") Airborne Division (a unit that counted Maxwell Taylor and William Westmoreland among its previous commanders) began arriving at the end of July. Small contingents of Australian and New Zealand troops also began to arrive in that summer. President Johnson laid great stress on getting other allies to send troops to fight in Vietnam; eventually 15 Pacific nations sent small military or technical contingents, the largest—and most feared by the Vietnamese—coming from South Korea. Other branches of the U.S. military swung into action. B-52 bombers based in Guam began bombing Communist troop concentrations in South Vietnam for the first time, and U.S. destroyers offshore began shelling inland targets.

In late June 1965 General Westmoreland received formal authorization to commit American forces to battle whenever necessary "to strengthen the relative position of [South Vietnamese] forces." The growing numbers of U.S. forces and the change in their mission was soon reflected in their casualty rates. In the first three months of 1965, 71 Americans were killed in Vietnam; in the last three months of the same year 920 were killed. The new reality of the war was that it was the Americans who would do the serious fighting in the jungles and rice paddies. The ARVN troops, so prone to military disaster whenever sent into the field, would for the most part be kept in various forms of guard duty. Not that this kept them from being frequently bloodied by Viet Cong attacks, with ARVN soldiers dying at a rate of about 1,000 a month in 1966 and 1967.

The U.S. decision to send in ground combat troops apparently took the Communists by surprise. A captured North Vietnamese document dated March 5, 1965, the day before the marines landed at Da Nang, rated the possibility of American troops being dispatched "to become the primary force to fight us" in South Vietnam as "small":

> They would have to make enormous expenditures in money and material, but would still not be certain of victory, and if they were defeated, they would lose even more face. As for us, if they send U.S. troops, there will be new difficulties and complexities but we will be determined to fight protractedly and, finally, victory will be ours.

As George Ball had predicted, North Vietnam was matching the U.S. escalation of the war with counterescalations of its own. Men and arms poured down the Ho Chi Minh trail. In April the CIA reported the presence of the crack 325th Division of the North Vietnamese army inside South Vietnam, a "most ominous" development, in the CIA's assessment. In early April 1965 Johnson declared in a speech at Johns Hopkins University that the United States was ready to engage in "unconditional discussions" to end the war. The North Vietnamese refused, calling instead for the implementation of the 1954 Geneva accords, which would have required the withdrawal of American forces from South Vietnam. By mid-1965 both the United States and North Vietnam were settling in for a long and bloody conflict.

7

THE "GRUNTS"

Every American war seems to bring forth a new name for those who risk their lives in the front lines. In World War I the soldiers who fought in the American Expeditionary Force in France were called "doughboys." In World War II the soldiers who fought in Europe and the Pacific were called "GIs." In Vietnam, both soldiers and marines came to be known by a single, simple name, "grunts." Too often in remembering wars, the best-known names are those of famous generals. But no general, no matter how brilliant or courageous, would live in the pages of history were it not for the sacrifices of the common foot soldiers under his command. The top-secret documents revealed in the Pentagon Papers provide the best view of the war as seen through the eyes of the generals and civilian policy-makers who wrote the orders in Washington. The personal letters collected in a 1985 book, *Dear America: Letters Home from Vietnam,* offer the best view of the war as seen through the eyes of the grunts whose job it was to carry out those orders in Vietnam.

Some of the men destined to fight in Vietnam, especially in the early days of the war, went off to battle with an almost exalted sense of mission. A marine, Pfc. Richard E. Marks, for example, sent his parents a "Last Will & Testament" soon after he arrived in Vietnam in 1965, reprinted in *Dear America:*

> I am here because I have always wanted to be a Marine and because I always wanted to see combat. I don't like being over here, but I am doing a job that must be done—I am fighting an inevitable enemy that

must be fought—now or later. I am fighting to protect and maintain what I believe in and what I want to live in—a democratic society. If I am killed while carrying out this mission, I want no one to cry or mourn for me. I want people to hold their heads high and be proud of me for the job I did.

Marks would be killed in action two months later.

Others, like army Sp4c. Robert Devlin, took a more matter-of-fact attitude about being sent to Vietnam. He wrote to his father in April 1967, telling him that his unit had just gotten orders to ship out:

Our company commander and our battalion and brigade commanders told us that there is no sense trying to fool ourselves, we are going for sure. The only thing that makes me mad is how do they expect you to tell your parents. They act as though it is an everyday experience, and that we should feel that way. I don't mind going, but there are some guys here who just won't make it, and I don't think they will make it out alive.

Devlin survived his year of combat in Vietnam.

More than 3 million men served in the Vietnam War. Although that is a large number, those who wound up fighting represented only a minority of their generation. All told, nearly 27 million men came of draft age (18 to 26) during the Vietnam War. Of these, more than 2 million were drafted, while nearly 9 million enlisted in the armed forces. The remainder were spared the possibility of going to Vietnam through deferments, evasion, disqualifications, or some other means, such as joining the National Guard. Due to college deferments from the draft, high school dropouts or graduates who had not gone on to college were twice as likely to serve in the military as college graduates. That meant that the military in Vietnam was composed, in large measure, of poor and working-class teenagers; the average age of a combat soldier in Vietnam was 19 years, compared to the average 26 years of age of soldiers in World War II. More than 3,000 of America's dead in Vietnam were 18 or younger when they died. Minorities also accounted for a share of combat soldiers and combat deaths far out of proportion to their numbers in the general population. African Americans, who made up 11 percent of the U.S. population, represented more than 20 percent of battlefield deaths in 1965–66. That percentage declined somewhat in later years as the army and marines took measures to equalize the dangers.

THE "GRUNTS"

Many of those who enlisted rather than waiting to be drafted or seeking deferments did so out of a sense of patriotism. Others did so knowing that enlistment allowed them to choose which branch of the military they would serve in, and which jobs they would train for in the military. Those choices could determine whether they lived or died in Vietnam; an enlisted man in the air force or the navy had a much better chance of escaping death or injury in Vietnam than one in the army or marines.

Even in the army and the marines, not everyone was at equal risk. The U.S. war effort in Vietnam depended upon a huge "rear echelon" of men engaged in noncombat functions, such as supply and transport and administration. In 1967 only 14 percent of the troops in Vietnam (fewer than 80,000) were actually assigned to combat, compared to 39 percent of all troops assigned to combat in World War II. It was the draftees who usually ended up carrying a rifle in the infantry; in 1969 they accounted for 62 percent of all American battlefield deaths in Vietnam.

The army supplied the majority of fighting men in the American war effort in Vietnam. Seven infantry divisions, four independent infantry brigades, and an armored cavalry regiment were deployed in Vietnam. The marines deployed two divisions and a number of smaller specialized units, including a marine aircraft wing. The Seventh Air Force Command, made up of four fighter wings and other supporting groups, was responsible for U.S. Air Force operations controlled by the Strategic

U.S. Navy river craft patrol the Mekong Delta. *(U.S. Army)*

Air Command from bases in Guam, Thailand, and Okinawa. The navy operated at sea, with carriers, battleships, cruisers, destroyers, and other vessels, and on South Vietnam's inland waters with the smaller vessels of its River Patrol Force and Riverine Assault Force; navy pilots flew missions over North and South Vietnam, Laos, and Cambodia.

Military strategists in Saigon divided South Vietnam into four regions. I Corps (pronounced "eye core") Tactical Zone in the north, headquartered in Da Nang, was home for much of the war to the Marine Corps's First and Third Divisions, and the army's Americal Division, later reinforced by the army's First Cavalry Division and 101st Airborne, and the Third Brigade of the Eighty-second Airborne. II Corps ("two core") Tactical Zone in the central region, headquartered at Pleiku, was home to the First Cavalry Division, the Fourth Infantry Division, and the 173rd Airborne Brigade, as well as Special Forces units. III Corps Tactical Zone in the area around Saigon, headquartered in Bien Hoa, was also home at various times to the 173rd Airborne Brigade, the First and Twenty-fifth Infantry Divisions, and the First Cavalry Division. The IV Corps Tactical Zone in the Mekong Delta region, headquartered at Can Tho, was home to the Ninth Infantry Division and Special Forces units.

More than 7,500 women also served in Vietnam in the military, most in the Army Nurse Corps, but also as administrators, advisers to ARVN's Women's Army Corps, and in other jobs. Eight American servicewomen died in Vietnam—seven army nurses and one air force nurse. Women also served as civilian volunteers working for the Red Cross, the United Service Organizations (USO), and other agencies. In April 1975, 37 civilian American women were killed when the air force transport plane evacuating them from Saigon crashed.

The war in South Vietnam was ultimately an infantryman's war, though more specialized units also played a role. Although a number of airborne units were assigned to Vietnam, as well as airborne personnel assigned to U.S. Marine reconnaissance battalions and the U.S. Army Special Forces, paratroopers wound up making only a couple of combat parachute jumps during the war. Like other units, the airborne units were usually carried into battle by helicopter.

Both the army and the marines had tank battalions deployed in Vietnam. Tanks, like the M-48 Patton, were at first thought to be out of their natural element in Vietnam's jungles and hilly terrain, but some units made good use of them in providing support to the infantry in

The first five enlisted women in the Women's Air Force (WAF) and the fourth WAF officer to be assigned to Vietnam arrive at Tan Son Nhut Air Base, South Vietnam. *(National Archives)*

combat. The M-551 Sheridan, a light tank with complicated electronic controls, proved too vulnerable to South Vietnam's damp and heat—and to Viet Cong land mines—to do much good. The M-113 Armored Personnel Carrier (APC) was used in many combat operations by both Americans and South Vietnamese ARVN troops.

The standard infantry weapon carried by Americans in Vietnam was the lightweight M-16 rifle, firing 5.56-mm cartridges, which could be used as a single-shot or fully automatic weapon, with an effective range of 400 to 500 yards. Introduced in 1967, early models of the M-16 were plagued with defects that cost some soldiers their lives in firefights and led to a congressional investigation. The infantry was also equipped with heavier weapons, such as M-60 machine guns, M-79 grenade launchers, and M-72 light antitank weapons. Supporting fire for the infantry could include artillery fire, helicopter gunships, fighter-bombers, and battleships and destroyers supporting coastal operations. Specially outfitted U.S. Air Force transport planes like the C-47 and C-119 also lent their firepower to the infantry in battles with the enemy. Equipped with Gatling guns capable of firing 6,000 rounds per

A flame tank sprays napalm, 1968. *(U.S. Marine Corps)*

minute, these fixed-wing gunships were called "Spooky" and "Puff, the Magic Dragon" by appreciative grunts on the ground.

Among those who fought the war on the ground, there were some units and individuals who had particularly dangerous assignments. The men of the Long Range Reconnaissance Patrols (LRRP)—called "lurps" by the grunts—would spend days or even weeks in enemy-controlled territory, gathering information and conducting raids and special missions. Then there were the "tunnel rats," who volunteered to explore and flush out the enemy from the large systems of underground tunnels the Viet Cong dug as living quarters, warehouses, and hospitals. In the "Iron Triangle" region north of Saigon alone, the Viet Cong had dug some 125 miles of tunnels by 1965. "These people are like moles," a sergeant with the Americal Division wrote home in 1969. "They can dig miles of tunnel but there is no dirt to be found anywhere. They must eat it." Tunnel rats had to watch out for booby traps, bats, scorpions, and Viet Cong soldiers who sometimes lay in wait for them in the dark around the next turn.

More than half the Americans who died in combat in Vietnam were killed by small-arms fire, reflecting Viet Cong reliance on ambush tactics and close-up small unit engagements. This contrasts with World War II and the Korean War, where most soldiers were killed by artillery fire.

Another great danger in Vietnam was the presence of booby traps sown by the Viet Cong, including mines, grenades, and sharpened bamboo "pungi" stakes in camouflaged pits; 11 percent of all American battlefield deaths were caused by such devices, compared to less than 4 percent in World War II. Army lieutenant Robert Ransom, Jr., wrote to his parents in 1968 describing his newfound "respect" for the Viet Cong:

> He knows that he can't stand up to us in a fire fight due to our superior training, equipment and our vast arsenal of weapons. Yet he is able. Via his mines and booby traps, he can whittle our ranks down . . . In the month that I have been with the company, we have lost 4 killed and about 30 wounded. We have not seen a single verified dink [enemy soldier] the whole time, nor have we even shot a single round at anything.

Ransom himself died a month later from wounds suffered when he was hit by shrapnel from a Viet Cong mine.

The number of Americans killed in Vietnam would have climbed much higher than it did had it not been for the high standards of care provided by the military medical services. In particular, aerial evacuation of the wounded by helicopters called "medevacs" or "dustoffs" saved many lives; the percentage of American casualties who died after reaching medical facilities dropped from 4.5 percent during World War II to 2.6 percent in the Vietnam War.

All wars have their blunders, tragedies, and senseless sacrifices, which can leave fighting troops with feelings of frustration and futility. But Vietnam was a particularly difficult war for the men who fought it to comprehend. Unlike the doughboys of World War I and the GIs of World War II, the grunts in Vietnam had no clearly defined objectives to capture. After some debate, U.S. military leaders in Saigon settled upon a strategy for fighting the war they called "search and destroy." Rather than attempting to capture and hold onto particular stretches of territory, General Westmoreland kept his troops continually on the move, probing, patrolling, seeking out the enemy in South Vietnam's forests, jungles, and mountain ranges.

Sometimes intelligence reports, from reconnaissance flights or civilian informers, pinpointed the exact location of an enemy unit. Then the fighter-bombers and the big B-52s from Guam or Thailand could pile on the Viet Cong and North Vietnamese forces with bombs, rockets, and napalm, followed by ground troops delivered by helicopter to landing zones (LZs) nearby. But more often, soldiers and marines had to pull on their packs and "hump the boonies," endlessly patrolling the backcountry seeking out the enemy. That was the "searching" part of search and destroy. When contact was made—usually at the initiative of the Viet Cong or North Vietnamese—and the patrolling Americans were in a firefight with the enemy, then the grunts could call in artillery support from nearby fire bases, and air support, and with luck carry out the "destroying" part of search and destroy. This was a strategy of attrition, of gradually wearing down the enemy's ability to continue the war by killing more and more of his fighters.

Search-and-destroy operations killed a lot of enemy soldiers. But they also left the grunts feeling like their role in the war was to serve as bait for the enemy. Once they had marched up a mountain slope or through a jungle and found the enemy, they usually had nothing to show for their efforts, except, perhaps, a favorable "kill ratio"—meaning that many more Viet Cong and North Vietnamese were killed than

General William C. Westmoreland, commander of Military Assistance Command, Vietnam, from 1964 to1968 *(U.S. Army)*

THE "GRUNTS"

A search-and-destroy mission *(U.S. Army Military History Institute)*

Americans. When the battle was over, the grunts returned to their base camps, and there was nothing to prevent the remaining enemy soldiers from moving right back up the mountain or into the jungle they had just been driven from.

The search-and-destroy strategy, meanwhile, conflicted with the other stated mission of the United States in Vietnam, which was to help "win the hearts and minds" of the South Vietnamese people away from the Communists. How were they to win the hearts or minds of people whom they were either ordered, or came on their own, to treat as part of the enemy? When the grunts were sent on search-and-destroy missions in enemy-held territory, part of what they usually wound up destroying were the homes, belongings and food supplies of the local villagers. They used their cigarette lighters to burn down the thatched huts of the villagers, in what became known as "Zippo raids." Whole sections of South Vietnam were declared free-fire zones where the infantry, artillery, and air forces were authorized to shoot at anything that moved, since the area was thought to be controlled by the Communists. The civilians killed as a result were added to the "body count" of enemy dead, the military's chief statistical measure of progress in the war.

An American lieutenant is treated by a medic after his leg is burned by an exploding Viet Cong white phosphorus booby trap. *(National Archives)*

Of course, some Vietnamese civilians—men, women, and children alike—did aid the Viet Cong, by reporting on American movements, storing weapons and ammunition, or placing booby traps. Warren Wooten, an 18-year-old marine private first class in Vietnam from 1965 to 1966, recalled years later:

> It seemed like the whole country was an enemy. The animals, the reptiles, the insects, the plants. And the people—you just couldn't respect 'em anymore. You knew they were going, "Eh, GI Number One," during the day, but at night they were trying to kill you.

And few Americans felt at home in Vietnam or comfortable with Vietnamese people. Army Private First Class John Dabonka, writing to his parents in December 1966, shortly after arrival in South Vietnam, complained:

Bob Kerrey and America's Haunted Memory

BOB KERREY'S LIFE IS AN EXAMPLE OF HOW, DECADES afterward, the Vietnam War continues to haunt Americans. Kerrey went to Vietnam as a 25-year-old lieutenant in a navy SEAL unit. In March 1969, two months after he arrived, he lost his right leg below the knee to a Viet Cong grenade on a mission for which he earned a Medal of Honor. In later years he enjoyed a successful career as a politician. He was a senator from Nebraska. Retiring from the U.S. Senate in 2000, he became president of the New School for Social Research in New York City in 2001.

That was before his life was turned upside down in 2001 by news reports of his possible involvement in a wartime atrocity. Shortly before midnight on February 25, 1969, Kerrey led a raid by seven navy SEALs on Thanh Phong, a village in the Mekong Delta. Kerrey's commando raiders hoped to capture or kill local Viet Cong leaders. Instead, they found only old men, women, and children. According to the testimony of Gerhard Klann, a 20-year SEAL veteran, the Americans murdered more than a dozen unarmed villagers.

Kerrey disputed Klann's account. His men, he said, had come under fire and had shot back in self-defense. But he acknowledged that only unarmed civilians had been killed—even though in 1969 he had reported to the navy that his men had killed 21 Viet Cong fighters that night. He admitted that he should not have accepted the Bronze Star he received for heroism at Thanh Phong. Whatever really happened that night, Kerrey was ashamed of his actions: "I thought dying for your country was the worst thing that could happen to you, and I don't think it is. I think killing for your country can be a lot worse. Because that's the memory that haunts."

The people live like pigs. They don't know how to use soap. When they have to go to the bathroom, they go wherever they're standing, they don't care who is looking.

Sp4c. John R. Riggan, a medic with the army's First Infantry Division, wrote his parents early in 1969 to complain about the attitude toward the Vietnamese displayed by so many of his fellow Americans. The Americans were:

cursed by a generalized inability to view these people whom we "came to save" as equals. First, they must have clean towns, nice cars, TV sets, and Western clothes before we will accept them as being almost our peers . . . A Vietnamese remains a "gook" no matter whose side he's on.

Another strange aspect of the war in Vietnam was that soldiers were not expected to remain at war until final victory came. Enlisted men were sent to Vietnam for a 12-month tour of duty, which meant that their "DEROS" (or "Date Eligible to Return from Overseas" in military jargon) was always on their mind. Particularly as their tour neared its end and they were "short," the grunts' morale suffered. No one wanted to risk getting wounded or killed with only a few days or weeks remaining before they could return to "the World," as life outside of Vietnam was referred to. Officers also served 12-month tours but rotated

U.S. Marines treat a wounded 15-year-old North Vietnamese soldier captured during fighting near Cam Lo, a village just south of the demilitarized zone, July 22, 1966. *(National Archives)*

THE "GRUNTS"

A Sky Trooper from the First Cavalry Division (Airmobile) keeps track of the time he has left to serve in Vietnam on his "short time" helmet. *(National Archives)*

through combat command positions even more quickly, often staying in a given command for six months or less. The military liked such rapid rotations, because it gave more officers a chance to "punch their ticket" with a tour of combat duty, a plus in terms of future promotion possibilities. But the practice undercut the stability and knowledge of combat commanders: Inexperienced commanders lost more men in battle than those with greater combat experience.

Every American soldier who fought in Vietnam was guaranteed at least a week off from the war for "rest and rehabilitation," or R&R. Servicemen could spend their R&R at special sites in Vietnam like China Beach, or travel to Hawaii, Bangkok, Hong Kong, Manila, and other Pacific cities. R&R was intended, like the one-year tour of duty, to boost morale. But many men found it disorienting to shift from combat to vacation and back again. Lt. Robert Santos, a highly decorated veteran of the 101st Airborne, described his visit to China Beach in a letter home in 1968:

> Since I've been here I haven't seen a bed till my R&R. I've taken one shower in two months, wore the same clothes for two months, and have been sleeping on the ground in water. I guess that's why they say war is hell—cause people in hell don't even get wet. Right now I'm sitting on a veranda overlooking the ocean, watching the waves break on the shore beneath me, and in 24 hours I'll be back out fighting the NVA [North Vietnamese Army].

Walter Mack, commander of a marine rifle company from 1967 to 1968, recalled years later that when he went on R&R, all the "toughness" he had developed in the field "dissipated":

> I was eating well and sleeping well. I called home . . . We talked about when I'd get home, what we'd do together, where I'd live. I bought some suits, spent some money on presents for people.

Returning to the field, with only 30 days left in his tour of duty, he could not help thinking that he "might never go home. I might never see those people again. I might never get a chance to enjoy those suits."

Once in Vietnam, few of the grunts talked much about defending the free world or keeping the dominoes from toppling. Even though they were not the best-led soldiers in history, the grunts fought hard and bravely. In his memoir, *A Soldier Reports,* General Westmoreland called the Americans in Vietnam "the finest military force . . . ever assembled," a judgment that—at least until a serious deterioration in morale set in after the spring of 1968—was not completely farfetched. But what kept the grunts going was not a complicated ideology or even a simple love of country as much as it was a loyalty to the buddies they fought alongside. Surviving the war, and seeing to it that your buddies survived, meant killing the enemy before he killed you. The grunts'-eye-view of the war was perhaps best expressed by a marine lieutenant named Victor Westphall, who shared the lives and sufferings of his men until he was killed in an ambush in May 1968. Writing his brother shortly before his death, he described a search-and-destroy operation in the midst of monsoon season, where nothing seemed to go right:

THE "GRUNTS"

We were all in sad shape now. I know that at one point, my feet about to crack open, my stomach knotted by hunger and diarrhea, my back feeling like a mirror made of nerves shattered in a million pieces by my flak jacket, pack, and extra mortars and machine-gun ammo, my hands a mass of hamburger from thorn cuts, and my face a mass of welts from mosquitoes, I desired greatly to throw down everything, slump into the water of a paddy, and sob. I remember a captain, an aviator, who, observing a group of grunts toasting the infantry in a bar, said, "You damned infantry think you're the only people who exist." You're damned right we do.

8

GROUND WAR

◆━◈━━━━━━━━━━━━━━━━━━━━━━━━━━

1965–1967

In the spring of 1965 the U.S.-backed government in Saigon and the war against Communists in South Vietnam tottered on the edge of collapse. The military strongmen who followed one another in and out of power in the year and a half after Diem's assassination enjoyed little support among their countrymen. They were unable to rally the South Vietnamese armed forces to stand effectively against the ever-more-powerful combination of Viet Cong guerrillas and North Vietnamese regulars in the countryside. Lyndon Johnson's advisers warned him that drastic steps would be needed to prevent the fall of South Vietnam to the Communists.

After months of indecision, Johnson acted decisively, ordering American bombers to attack North Vietnam and dispatching American ground combat forces into South Vietnam. Those decisions, plus the fact that a more stable (if not particularly popular) government came to power in Saigon under the joint leadership of Gen. Nguyen Van Thieu and Air Vice Marshal Nguyen Cao Ky, saved South Vietnam for the moment from Communist takeover. The search-and-destroy operations ordered by General Westmoreland, American commander in South Vietnam, bled the Communist forces. But in the end the impressive "body counts" and "kill ratios" racked up by American troops in those operations did not hamper the Communists' willingness and ability to continue the war indefinitely. American firepower proved no substitute for a genuinely popular and effective South Vietnamese government.

GROUND WAR

U.S. Marines engage in a firefight with the North Vietnamese army near a secondary treeline, 1968. *(U.S. Marine Corps)*

The first full-scale battles between American and Communist ground forces went well for the United States, seeming to promise a turn in the fortunes of war. In August 1965 U.S. Marines trapped a Viet Cong regiment on the Bantangan Peninsula, near the new marine air base at Chu Lai. This was the first major ground action in which U.S. troops were deployed to fight on their own without their South Vietnamese allies. After the marines blocked the Viet Cong retreat from the peninsula, the enemy force was bombarded from the air and sea. Nearly 700 were killed. Shortly afterward, the U.S. Army's newly arrived First Air Cavalry Division took on North Vietnamese regulars for the first time. The Air Cav was sent by General Westmoreland to relieve the defenders of a besieged Special Forces camp at Plei Me in the Central Highlands. Air Cav troopers drove off the enemy, inflicting heavy casualties. Although it was too soon to proclaim that final victory was in sight, Adm. U. S. Grant Sharp, commander of military forces in the Pacific, declared in a press interview in Honolulu in late October 1965 that the United States and South Vietnam had "stopped losing" the war.

The most fiercely fought engagement of American and Communist forces in 1965 came the following month in the Ia Drang Valley. The Communists driven off from Plei Me redeployed in the Ia Drang Valley below a mountainous region known as the Chu Pong near the Cambodian border. There they were reinforced by fresh troops from the north. Meanwhile soldiers from the First Air Cav continued to hunt for the Communists.

On November 14, about 450 soldiers from the First Battalion of the Seventh Cavalry made a helicopter landing in the Ia Drang Valley. (The Seventh, part of the First Air Cavalry, was descended from the horse cavalry unit that met its fate under the command of Gen. George Custer at the Battle of the Little Bighorn in the Indian wars.) They did not meet any opposition when they landed at about 11 A.M. All went well for the first hour on the ground, until soldiers from one platoon ran into the North Vietnamese. The Americans then came under heavy assault from automatic weapons, mortars, and rocket-propelled grenades. They soon found themselves surrounded and taking heavy casualties. In hand-to-hand combat, the hard-pressed troopers beat back their attackers. The two sides were so close together that a U.S. Air Force jet mistakenly dropped napalm on an American position. After the battle was over, an American and a North Vietnamese soldier were found lying dead, side by side; the American still had his hands gripped tightly around the throat of his enemy. Second Lieutenant Walter Marm, Jr., won the Medal of Honor that day for single-handedly attacking and killing all of an eight-man North Vietnamese machine-gun crew.

Enemy ground fire was too intense for relief to come from the air until after dark. Reinforcements from the Second Battalion of the Fifth Cavalry had to be landed several miles away; they fought their way through on land to relieve the Seventh the following day. But the relief force was as hard hit as the soldiers they were coming to aid. Jack Smith, part of the relief force, provided a vivid account of the intensity of the battle in a magazine article published some months afterward:

> Our artillery and air strikes started coming in. Just before they started, I could hear North Vietnamese voices . . . The Skyraiders were dropping napalm bombs a hundred feet in front of me on a [North Vietnamese] machine gun complex. I felt the hot blast and saw the elephant grass curling ahead of me. The victims were screaming . . . No matter what you did, you got hit. The snipers in the trees just waited for someone to

move, then shot him . . . I don't know why, but when a man is hit in the belly, he screams an unearthly scream. Something you cannot imagine; you actually have to hear it. When a man is hit in the chest or the belly, he keeps on screaming, sometimes until he dies. I just lay there, numb, listening to the bullets whining over me and the 15 or 20 men close to me screaming and screaming and screaming.

Smith's unit suffered heavy casualties. At one point in the battle, North Vietnamese troops walked through the American position, killing the wounded Americans where they lay. Smith, covered with blood from his own wounds, played dead and survived.

The North Vietnamese finally broke off their attack on November 15. For the next few days they were pounded by B-52 bombings, and several smaller ground battles were fought between the two sides until the battle finally ended on November 18. The North Vietnamese pulled out of the Ia Drang Valley, some of them moving across the border into Cambodia. Lt. Gen. Harry W. O. Kinnard, commander of the First Cavalry Division (Air Mobile), requested permission to follow the enemy into Cambodia (which was, officially, a neutral country), but permission was denied by Washington. Kinnard complained bitterly after the war that his soldiers had not been able to pursue the enemy across the border into Cambodia, Laos, or North Vietnam "even in hot pursuit":

A 1966 battle—the marine to the far right is firing an M-16, the standard American rifle after 1966. (*U.S. Marine Corps*)

Short of that, I didn't see how it was going to be possible to keep the guerrillas from being reinforced at will. It was pretty clear that if you can't quarantine the area where the guerrillas are, it's very unlikely you're really going to pressure them . . . So you kept butting your head against the reality of a war where you have a fifty-yard line and you're told to play your game on one side of it. The other guy's able to play where you are, but you can't go where he is. At best that's a long-term stalemate, and our people aren't good at that.

Although the United States was already openly bombing North Vietnam, and secretly bombing Laos, and the CIA was conducting a secret war in Laos with U.S.-armed Meo tribesmen, President Johnson refrained from attacks on Cambodia. Under President Nixon the U.S. government began a secret bombing campaign in Cambodia in 1969, and openly sent in ground troops in the May 1970 "incursion."

Four days of battle in the Ia Drang Valley resulted in the deaths of 230 Americans and perhaps 1,300 North Vietnamese. As a direct result of this battle, the Communists abandoned plans to launch an offensive through the Central Highlands that would have split South Vietnam in two. Smarting from their losses in the Ia Drang Valley, the Communists avoided further major conflicts with the Americans for the remainder of 1965. The escalated war was getting off to a good start in the eyes of American leaders. General Westmoreland proudly declared in his memoirs that "in the Highlands as on the Bantangan Peninsula, the American fighting man and his commanders had performed without the setbacks that have sometimes marked first performances in other wars." Westmoreland made an even larger claim in his memoirs:

From this beginning until American withdrawal some seven and a half years later no American unit in South Vietnam other than a few companies on the offensive or an occasional small outpost ever incurred what could fairly be called a setback. This is a remarkable record.

To control the battlefield after an engagement and to kill more of the enemy than he killed of your forces was, by Westmoreland's definition, an American victory. For the enemy to abandon the battlefield and suffer heavier casualties than the Americans was by the same logic a Communist "setback." Perhaps that was an adequate definition of victory and defeat in other wars—but not in this one. The Communists of South and

North Vietnam were prepared to fight a very long war against the Americans (as they had against the French before them). It was certainly true that with the arrival of the Americans, the Communists were forced to abandon their hopes for achieving such strategic military objectives as splitting South Vietnam in two. But what Communist leaders realized was that the very act of continuing the war was in itself a strategic victory. In the long run, the 230 American dead in the Ia Drang Valley (and the tens of thousands more who would soon die) weighed more heavily in the balance of victory and defeat than the 1,300 North Vietnamese who died in those four days (and the hundreds of thousands more Communist dead to come). By the end of 1965, there were 184,300 U.S. troops in South Vietnam, an increase of 161,000 from the end of 1964. The United States had by now suffered a total of 1,636 killed in the war, 1,369 of whom had died since the start of 1965.

The years 1966 and 1967 were the high point of U.S. search-and-destroy operations. The biggest operations included Operation Masher (later renamed White Wing at Lyndon Johnson's insistence, for public relations reasons). Masher/White Wing ran from late January through March 1966, on the Bong Son Plain in Central Vietnam, resulting in a body count of 2,389 enemy dead. Operation Hastings, involving troops from the U.S. Marines and the ARVN, ran from mid-July to early August 1966 in Quang Tri province below the demilitarized zone (DMZ) dividing South and North Vietnam. This operation produced a body count of more than 800 North Vietnamese troops. It was followed up immediately by another marine operation, code-named Prairie, which ran from early August through mid-September with a body count of more than 1,000 enemy dead. The army's Operation Attleboro, which ran from mid-October through late November 1966 in Tay Ninh province near the Cambodian border, resulted in a body count of 1,100 enemy dead.

The year 1967 opened with Operation Cedar Falls in the "Iron Triangle" stronghold of the Viet Cong north of Saigon. The U.S. Army claimed a body count of 700 enemy dead. As a result of journalist Jonathan Schell's magazine articles and later book, *The Village of Ben Suc,* this operation became notorious for its strategy of destroying Vietnamese villages and forcibly resettling their inhabitants. Large stretches of forest in the Iron Triangle were destroyed by army engineers driving specially designed bulldozers known as Rome Plows. Operation Junction City began in February 1967 and lasted through May. This was the largest single American operation of the war. It was staged in War Zone C, northwest of Saigon along the Cambodian border, and was designed to capture the Communist command center in South Vietnam (known as COSVN to U.S. military strategists). The 30,000 troops involved failed to find the site of COSVN, but the operation produced a body count of nearly 3,000 enemy dead.

Some of the big search-and-destroy operations of 1966 to 1967 were joint South Vietnamese–American efforts, but for the most part, the Americans were now taking the place of their allies in combat. With the exception of some elite South Vietnamese battalions of airborne troops and marines, ARVN earned a reputation for engaging in "search-and-evade" missions when its units were sent into the field. Reviewing the statistical performance of the Eighteenth ARVN Division, which claimed to have conducted 5,237 patrols in one week in 1966, during which it made a total of only 13 contacts with the enemy, U.S. adviser John Paul Vann wrote disgustedly, "I can easily establish more enemy contacts on a daily basis myself."

Marines from a U.S. Seventh Fleet ready group and an interpreter from the Republic of Vietnam army talk with a village elder during Operation Daggerthrust, 1966. The elder tells them about Viet Cong troops in the area. *(National Archives)*

As the French had learned in the first Indochina war, Communist guerrilla fighters were hard to find, unless they wanted to be found. The Communists were almost always tipped off in advance of American plans, either through their own spies or air and artillery strikes. A study by the U.S. Army showed that from 1966 to 1967 the overwhelming majority of all battles in South Vietnam were started by the Communists, usually when they ambushed American units in the countryside. According to Shelby Stanton, a military historian and Vietnam veteran, "The American soldiers being fielded were simply green, and faring poorly as a result." It was not easy for them to learn the lessons they needed to learn if they were going to survive in a contest with experienced enemy guerrillas operating on their own home ground. The year-long "tour of duty" meant that combat-experienced American veterans were continually leaving South Vietnam, and newcomers (or "cherries" as they were called by more experienced grunts) were continually taking their place. If the "cherries" were lucky, they found someone to teach them what they needed to know before they got themselves killed. Angel Quintana, who served in Vietnam from 1966 to 1967 with the army's Fourth Division, recalled after the war:

> I saw a lot of battles. I can't even remember my first firefight, there were so many. After a while, you get used to it. They attack you and people die, and it's a normal thing . . . You learn to live in that world. And you watch the cherries come in, the replacements. Instead of carrying a combat pack, they have huge rucksacks. They're carrying shaving cream, aftershave, razors . . . a ton of stupid stuff. You see them on patrol trying to climb a hill, and they're sliding backward. Then you grab them and say, "Look. You can throw out the undershirts. You won't need them here. The underpants, too. And the clean socks. You don't take off your boots in combat."

Not all American military leaders shared General Westmoreland's enthusiasm for search-and-destroy operations. Marine Corps general Victor Krulak, commanding general of the Fleet Marine Force in the Pacific, had been an early and influential supporter of U.S. counterinsurgency efforts in South Vietnam. When the war was transformed by the introduction of U.S. ground combat forces, he began to have doubts about American strategy. Writing in December 1965, after the Ia Drang battle, he warned that the enemy was now "seeking to attrit [wear down by killing off] U.S. forces through the process of violent, close quarters combat which tends to diminish the effectiveness of our supporting arms." The Communists called this tactic "clinging to the belt," which meant that by staying close to their American opponents in battle they could prevent the U.S. forces from bringing their superior firepower (air strikes and artillery) into action.

Krulak argued that the Communists' hope for victory lay in inflicting enough U.S. casualties to "erode our national will and cause us to cease our support of the GVN [South Vietnam]." Westmoreland's strategy would wind up bleeding the enemy, but it would also bleed the Americans. American public opinion would not stand for as much bloodshed as the North Vietnam leadership was prepared to spend. As an alternative, Krulak called for renewed attention to pacification. If he had his way, the United States would be fighting a small-unit war, concentrating on securing territory and winning over the South Vietnamese people, rather than constantly trying to find and engage Hanoi's big units through ambitious search-and-destroy operations.

Vietnamese woman and children lie in a ditch with U.S. soldiers during Viet Cong attack on a military convoy, January 17, 1966.
(National Archives)

Westmoreland's obsession with the body counts generated by big search-and-destroy operations was counterproductive, in Krulak's view. Plastering the countryside with American bombs and shells was not the best way to win hearts and minds. "The raw figure of VC killed," he wrote to Defense Secretary Robert McNamara in 1966, "can be a dubious index of success since, if their killing is accompanied by devastation of friendly areas, we may end up having done more harm than good." The marines in I Corps, under the direct command of Gen. Lewis Walt, attempted to put Krulak's emphasis on pacification into operation in the heavily populated coastal strip in northern South Vietnam. But they did so in the face of opposition from Westmoreland and without support from Washington. Pacification efforts would be stepped up again in 1967, but continued to take second place to Westmoreland's search-and-destroy strategy.

No one knows how many Vietnamese civilians died in the Vietnam War. A U.S. Senate committee estimated 400,000 were killed and 900,000 wounded in South Vietnam alone. With large stretches of the South Vietnamese countryside turned into free-fire zones, millions of civilians fled their homes for the relative safety of the cities. Some American strategists welcomed this development, believing it would be more difficult for Communist guerrillas to function in a depopulated countryside. Neil Sheehan, a correspondent from the *New York Times,* asked General Westmoreland in 1966 about the number of civilians being unintentionally killed and wounded by American air strikes and artillery fire:

> Westmoreland is a courteous man, and he was forthcoming with the press during these early years of the American war . . . He looked at me carefully. "Yes, Neil, it is a problem," he said, "but it does deprive the enemy of the population, doesn't it?"

The war of attrition ground on in 1966–67. The Americans got better at killing the Viet Cong and North Vietnamese, but the enemy also got better at killing Americans. Search-and-destroy operations were driving the Communists from the center of the country, but they fought back on its edges. By the fall of 1967 the Communists were deliberately luring American units away from the heavily populated regions of South Vietnam. Their strategy was twofold: to continue to inflict casualties on the Americans, while clearing the way for a planned offensive in South Vietnam's cities the following year. In isolated corners of the country, they fought punishing battles with the Americans for control of meaningless

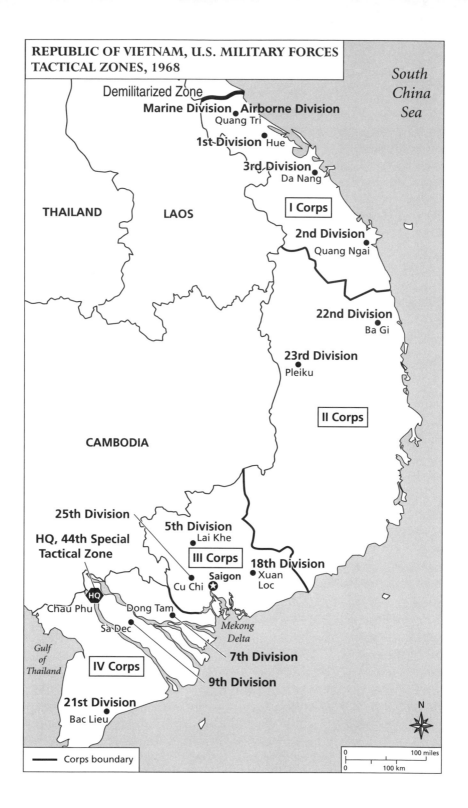

REPUBLIC OF VIETNAM, U.S. MILITARY FORCES TACTICAL ZONES, 1968

South China Sea

Demilitarized Zone

Marine Division • Airborne Division
Quang Tri

1st Division Hue

3rd Division
Da Nang

THAILAND

LAOS

I Corps

2nd Division
Quang Ngai

22nd Division
Ba Gi

23rd Division
Pleiku

II Corps

CAMBODIA

25th Division

5th Division
Lai Khe

HQ, 44th Special Tactical Zone

III Corps

18th Division
Xuan Loc

HQ
Chau Phu

Cu Chi

Saigon

Dong Tam

Sa Dec

Mekong Delta

Gulf of Thailand

IV Corps

7th Division

9th Division

21st Division
Bac Lieu

N

—— Corps boundary

| 0 | | 100 miles |
| 0 | 100 km | |

hilltops. The marines took heavy casualties in battles around Khe Sanh, near the Laotian border, and Con Thien, near the DMZ. The army, and particularly the 173rd Airborne, was hit hard in fighting near Dak To. In a four-day battle in mid-November for control of Hill 875, the 173rd lost 158 men. When the battle ended the Americans were left in control of the hill, and they had killed a great many of the enemy. Westmoreland declared that the battles around Dak To represented "the beginning of a great defeat for the enemy." But after the American "victory" of Hill 875, the hill was abandoned, like most of the hills and patches of jungle and rice paddy where Americans died that year. By the end of 1966, U.S. troop strength in Vietnam had increased to 385,300. Total U.S. deaths stood at 6,644. One year later U.S. troop strength had reached 485,600. The number of American dead had jumped to 16,021.

In his memoirs General Westmoreland would ridicule the "alleged genius" of his opponent, North Vietnamese military commander Vo Nguyen Giap: "A Western commander absorbing losses on the scale of Giap's would hardly have lasted in command more than a few weeks." In fact, Giap was relatively cautious. Unlike some North Vietnamese leaders who favored an all-out offensive in the South to bring victory in a short period, Giap believed in a more protracted military struggle, which would not be as costly in manpower. But there was no question that he was willing to spend the lives of his soldiers with what American commanders regarded as reckless abandon, if that was what it took to win. Giap explained to American journalist Stanley Karnow in 1990:

> We were not strong enough to drive out a half-million American troops, but that wasn't our aim. Our intention was to break the will of the American Government to continue the war. Westmoreland was wrong to expect that his superior firepower would grind us down. If we had focused on the balance of forces, we would have been defeated in two hours. We were waging a people's war . . . America's sophisticated arms, electronic devices and all the rest were to no avail in the end. In war there are the two factors—human beings and weapons. Ultimately, though, human beings are the decisive factor.

Giap's willingness to send hundreds of thousands of his soldiers to their deaths, and the willingness of his soldiers to fight on despite such heavy losses, would ultimately determine the outcome of the ground war in Vietnam.

9
AIR WAR

———◆——

The U.S. military could never be sure of its control of the ground during the war in Vietnam. A "pacified" village might harbor Viet Cong sympathizers who would report on American troop movements or plant booby traps to help the Communists. Jungles and hillsides might be honeycombed with the enemy's underground tunnels and bunkers. A trip down a peaceful-looking road could prove suicidal after dark. But Americans ruled the air over Vietnam with supreme confidence. Never before in the history of warfare had air power been used so extensively—to attack the enemy, to destroy enemy cover and food supplies, and to carry out dozens of other tasks. The lavish use of air power in Vietnam symbolized American technological know-how and material resources. In the end, though, statistics on numbers of missions flown and tons of bombs dropped were no more a guarantee of victory than were the body counts on the ground.

American pilots in Vietnam were an elite group; they were carefully selected, highly trained, and highly motivated. They had a wide array of the world's most sophisticated weapons at their disposal. Among the fighter-bombers employed in Vietnam was the air force's F-100 Super Sabre, which primarily provided air support for ground troops in South Vietnam. The F-105 Thunderchief—nicknamed "Thud" for the sound it was said to make when it crashed—was used by the air force extensively over North Vietnam. The navy and Marine Corps operated the A-4 Skyhawk and the A-6 Intruder. The B-52s of the air force's Strategic Air Command were also employed in both South and North Vietnam. The supersonic F-4 Phantom fighter served the air force, navy, and

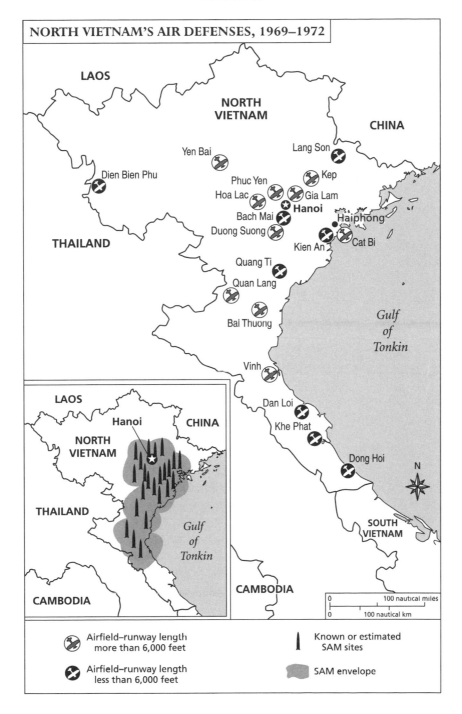

NORTH VIETNAM'S AIR DEFENSES, 1969–1972

marines, and shot down the majority of enemy planes (mostly Russian-
and Chinese-built MiGs over North Vietnam).

In South Vietnam, American air power was used to support the
ground troops in a variety of ways. Helicopters transported them into
battle zones and evacuated the wounded; gunships and fighter-bombers
hit enemy positions with machine-gun fire, bombs, rockets, and
napalm. One type of air support later came back to haunt many U.S.
soldiers. In 1962 the air force began to spray chemical defoliants in Vietnam, to kill off the vegetation that provided hiding places in jungles and
forests for Communist forces. In Operation Ranch Hand, specially
equipped C-123 cargo transport planes, flying just 150 feet above tree-
top level, sprayed the defoliating chemicals over the target zones. The
unofficial motto of the Ranch Hand pilots was "Only you can prevent
forests." They also used herbicides to destroy food crops that the Viet
Cong depended on. Twelve million gallons of a chemical spray called
Agent Orange, named after the color of the barrels in which it was
stored, were sprayed over South Vietnam.

In 1969 a scientific report linked Agent Orange, which contained a
poisonous chemical labeled 2,4,5-T (a type of dioxin), to birth defects
in laboratory animals. Critics of American policies in Vietnam worried
about Agent Orange's effects on members of the civilian population
who came in contact with the spray. Its use was ended in 1970. But it
was not only civilians who were at risk. American servicemen often
came in contact with Agent Orange, either on Ranch Hand crews or as
part of ground forces moving through areas sprayed with defoliants. In
the years following the Vietnam War, many veterans began developing
skin and liver diseases and cancer, or had children suffering from birth
defects. In 1982 a group of veterans who believed their health had been
damaged by Agent Orange sued the chemical companies that produced
the spray. The case was settled with an agreement by the companies to
establish a fund for Agent Orange victims.

The air war over North Vietnam was a major part of the American
strategy for victory. President Johnson's advisers believed that bombing
could bring North Vietnam's leaders to their knees; however, they were
not always in agreement as to how much would be required to do the
job. Military leaders complained of the restraints imposed on the
American bombing campaign. U.S. planes were not allowed to attack
the center of Hanoi, or the port of Haiphong, or the dikes that crisscrossed North Vietnam's richest agricultural lands. In the early months

This C-123 Ranch Hand aircraft sprays defoliant in areas near Tay Ninh and An Loc, South Vietnam. *(National Archives)*

of Operation Rolling Thunder, the bombing was concentrated on North Vietnam's transportation system: its roads, bridges, and railroads. President Johnson maintained tight personal control over the campaign, choosing many of the targets to be hit at regular Tuesday lunch meetings in the White House.

As the war dragged on, Johnson's civilian advisers, who favored limited bombing, gradually gave ground to military advocates of a more extensive attack. In 1966 U.S. bombers were allowed to hit oil and gas storage facilities and ammunition dumps, both previously off limits. In 1967 the permitted targets were again expanded to include airfields, power plants, and factories around North Vietnam's major cities of Hanoi and Haiphong. The number of sorties flown against the north jumped from 55,000 in 1965 to 148,000 the following year. (A sortie is a single mission flown by a single plane.) Total bomb tonnage dropped increased almost fourfold the same year. During the three and a half years of Operation Rolling Thunder, American pilots dropped an average of eight tons of explosives a day on North Vietnam. The bombing may have been "limited" but it was not light.

Policy makers in Washington thought of bombing as a "bargaining chip" in diplomacy. On several occasions Johnson stopped the bombing, to see if North Vietnam was willing to offer concessions in return.

The longest bombing halt ran from mid-December 1965 through January 1966. But the two sides remained far apart. The North Vietnamese would not negotiate unless the bombing was permanently ended; they also demanded that any peace settlement include the formation of a coalition government including the Viet Cong in Saigon. In 1967 Johnson stiffened the U.S. negotiating position, writing to Ho Chi Minh that the bombing would be suspended only if North Vietnam ended infiltration of troops and supplies into South Vietnam.

American pilots fought a very different kind of war than that experienced by the grunts in the jungles and rice paddies of South Vietnam. Navy radar intercept officer Pete Sillari, who flew missions over North Vietnam in the backseat of an F-4 Phantom, remembered the war as "very sterile and cool":

> I got in this little steel box that was as fast as the speed of sound. It was air-conditioned. I had all this high-tech equipment around me to get me back to my home steel box, where I had a hot shower and a hot meal, and then I'd get drunk every night. There was never any contact with people on the other side.

There was never any contact unless the pilot's plane happened to get shot down. "SAMs [surface-to-air missiles] connect you up with people on the ground," Sillari added, "and MiGs connect you up with people." With Soviet aid, the North Vietnamese set up a deadly system of antiaircraft defenses, including radar, antiaircraft guns, SAM batteries, and MiG-17 and MiG-21 fighters. Most of the U.S. planes lost over the North were shot down by SAMs or antiaircraft fire. But some were also lost in "dogfights" with enemy aircraft. The United States lost 92 planes in such fights, while shooting down 193 MiGs. The top American ace in the war, air force captain Charles DeBellevue, was credited with shooting down six MiGs. The best day's score was racked up by navy lieutenant Randy Cunningham and his radar interceptor officer, Lt. (jg) William Driscoll, who managed to down three MiG-17s in one day. The military made every effort to rescue downed pilots. The Air Forces Aerospace Rescue and Recovery Service specialized in going in with helicopters and amphibious planes to pick them up, often under enemy fire. Some 3,000 U.S. pilots were rescued during the war after being shot down.

Not all American airmen were so fortunate. The North Vietnamese regarded the more than 500 pilots they captured as "war criminals" and treated them very harshly, ignoring the Geneva Conventions for the protection of prisoners of war (POWs). Most POWs were initially taken to the Hao Lo Prison, which they dubbed the "Hanoi Hilton." That was a bitter joke, because the accommodations they found there were anything but hotel-like. Navy pilot Howard Rutledge, shot down over North Vietnam in November 1965, was told by his North Vietnamese interrogator, "You are not a prisoner of war. Your government has not declared war upon the Vietnamese people . . . You are protected by no international law." Rutledge was repeatedly tortured and was confined for six years alone in a windowless cell. Prisoners were tortured to extract confessions of "war crimes," and to break their will. Some found ways to resist. Navy commander Jeremiah Denton, brought before a press conference to testify to the good treatment the prisoners were receiving, spelled out the word *torture* by blinking his eyes in Morse code, a message decoded by CIA analysts watching news footage of the

U.S. Air Force Captain Wilmer N. Grubb is given first aid while being guarded by his captors in North Vietnam, January 1966. *(U.S. Air Force)*

The Hanoi Hilton

THE "HANOI HILTON," ORIGINALLY A FRENCH FORTRESS built in central Hanoi in the 19th century, was converted by the North Vietnamese into a prison for Americans captured during the Vietnam War. Its real name was Hoa Lo Prison; the Americans called it the "Hilton" as a grim joke. Prison facilities were primitive, and living quarters were infested with rats and insects. At the height of the war, about 360 Americans were held there, some in solitary confinement, others in crowded barracks rooms holding as many as 40 other men. Through 1969 the prisoners were treated with great brutality, including torture and beatings, before conditions improved due to international pressure brought to bear on North Vietnamese authorities. Jeremiah Denton, James Stockdale, and John S. McCain III were among the best known American POWs held there.

In the 1990s most of the prison was demolished to make way for two high-rise buildings, but a small section was preserved as a museum. Then in 1999 the real Hilton chain of hotels erected a luxury Hilton only a few blocks away—the final grim joke for those still around to appreciate it.

event. Torture of the POWs stopped after the autumn of 1969, perhaps in response to negative international publicity.

American pilots had orders to avoid civilian targets, and U.S. officials denied that any significant damage was being done to nonmilitary targets in North Vietnam. But whatever the official policy, many civilian population centers were hit by American bombs. Important targets in North Vietnam were guarded by batteries of guns and missiles. Twisting and turning wildly through the air to avoid enemy antiaircraft fire, fighter-bomber pilots could not always ensure that their bombs would land anywhere near the designated targets. When pilots for one or another reason could not find or hit their assigned target, they searched for other targets to hit instead. Capt. Randy Floyd, a marine pilot who flew bombing missions in North and South Vietnam in 1968, testified before Congress in 1972 about his experiences:

> If we found we had any ordnance [bombs] left or we tried to drop it and
> the ordnance did not drop, malfunctioned, there was an ordnance drop

zone fifty miles out to sea, but this was rarely used. Primarily it was used when you had ordnance that hung up and you wanted to go out and jettison it. But if you found no movers [moving targets], and you had bombs left after hitting the secondary target or something, or if you just felt like hitting something else, you would go and drop the bombs somewhere else, wherever you like in North Vietnam, in the target area.

Dick Rutan, a test pilot, flew air force F-100s over South and North Vietnam in 1967 and 1968, winning a Silver Star for his exploits. He later recalled his first flight into North Vietnam:

My first impression when we crossed the DMZ was that somebody had turned the goddamn place into the moon. I've never seen so many bomb craters in my whole life. I was appalled. And the thing that really got me was the city of Dong Hoi. It was the first major city north of the DMZ . . . You could see it was a fairly large town. But they had bombed that thing right into the Stone Age. All you could see was foundations. There was not a stick standing. Totally destroyed . . . And I thought— why in the world? Why did we do that?

Michael Maclear, a correspondent for the Canadian Broadcast Corporation, made a film documentary of the results of American bombing in North Vietnam in 1969. Traveling south along the heavily bombed Highway 1 in North Vietnam, Maclear found that five cities— Phu Ly, Ninh Binh, Thanh Hoa, Vinh, and Ha Tinh—had been "leveled" and others showed extensive bomb damage. So despite the official denials, civilian targets were hit often and hard in Operation Rolling Thunder and in later bombing campaigns. A CIA study in January 1967 estimated that 20,000 North Vietnamese (80 percent of them civilians) had lost their lives due to U.S. bombing. All told, between 1965 and 1973 an estimated 100,000 North Vietnamese civilians were killed by the bombing campaign.

Attacks on the civilian population united the North Vietnamese behind the war effort, just as German attacks on London during the Battle of Britain in World War II had stiffened the resistance of the English. And the material damage the bombing did to North Vietnam's capacity to wage war was limited. There just were not that many vital targets to hit in a largely agricultural nation like North Vietnam. Navy radar intercept officer Pete Sillari described the effect of U.S. bombing as one of moving "the dirt from the north side of the road to the south side. The next day we'd move the dirt from the south side of the road to the north side."

Even when they had an important target to aim at, American pilots found the bombing campaign difficult, dangerous, and too often futile. The Thanh Hoa bridge, 75 miles south of Hanoi, carried rail and road traffic, and was a vital link in North Vietnam's transportation system. It was first attacked on April 3, 1965, shortly after the start of Operation Rolling Thunder. Two U.S. planes were lost in the raid, which inflicted only minor damage on the bridge. Three planes were lost the next day (two of them to MiG fighters, the first air victories for North Vietnamese pilots). Over the next few years U.S. planes returned to the bridge dozens of times. And although dozens of planes were shot down, none ever succeeded in destroying the bridge, which became a symbol of North Vietnamese resistance.

The North Vietnamese went to great lengths to keep their transportation system rolling. Australian journalist Wilfred Burchett visited North Vietnam in 1966 and described the countermeasures that the North Vietnamese were taking to attacks on their bridges:

> Bamboo bridges would be lowered by winches at dawn and would be winched up at night for the truck convoys. And there were pontoons: half of a bridge would be on one bank of the river, the other half on the opposite bank, and they'd be floated out around dusk and put together. They reckoned that no bridge could be put out of action for more than four hours.

Hundreds of thousands of North Vietnamese laborers were mobilized to repair roads, bridges, and railroad lines struck by American bombers. Hanoi took other measures to minimize bomb damage, storing its oil in 50-gallon drums dispersed through the countryside rather than in large, vulnerable tanks. Bombing destroyed power plants, but the North Vietnamese switched to diesel-driven generators. North Vietnam's elaborate civil defense system included tunnels, trenches, bunkers, and concrete cylinders embedded in city streets and sidewalks, some only large enough for one person to hide in case of air raid.

A government-sponsored study by civilian scientists of the effects of the bombing in North Vietnam revealed that as of July 1966 "the U.S. bombing of North Vietnam had had no measurable direct effect on

John McCain
THE POW AS POPULAR POLITICIAN

THE STATUS OF "WAR HERO" HAS ALWAYS BEEN A plus for an aspiring politician. John F. Kennedy was one of the best-known World War II war heroes to go on to high elected office. The closest equivalent to Kennedy from the Vietnam War was probably John S. McCain III, a naval aviator and the son and grandson of navy admirals, who survived six years of brutal imprisonment in North Vietnam after his plane was shot down over Hanoi in 1967. Retiring from the navy in 1981, McCain won election as a congressional representative from Arizona the following year, and as a U.S. senator in 1986. He was a strong contender for the Republican presidential nomination in 2000. His status as a former POW also gave him added credibility when, in the Senate, he played a leading role in helping secure renewed diplomatic relations between the United States and the Socialist Republic of Vietnam.

Hanoi's ability to mount and support military operations in the South at the current level." North Vietnam's agricultural economy could not be significantly damaged by air attack; its transportation system could be easily rebuilt after attacks; and because most of the weapons being funneled down the Ho Chi Minh trail were supplied to North Vietnam from abroad, it made little difference how many North Vietnamese factories were destroyed. The experts concluded that even a vastly stepped-up bombing effort could not cut off the supply of troops and supplies from the north.

When Defense Secretary Robert McNamara read this report in the fall of 1966, it marked the beginning of his disillusionment with the war. Although publicly he continued to claim that Operation Rolling Thunder was a great success, privately he began to call for steps to scale down the war. In a memorandum for President Johnson drafted in mid-May 1967, McNamara warned:

> There may be a limit beyond which many Americans and much of the world will not permit the United States to go. The picture of the world's greatest superpower killing or seriously injuring 1,000 non-

combatants a week, while trying to pound a tiny backward nation into submission on an issue whose merits are hotly disputed, is not a pretty one. It could conceivably produce a costly distortion in the American national consciousness and in the world image of the United States.

Johnson ignored the memorandum, and McNamara decided soon afterward to resign as secretary of defense.

Infiltration of troops and supplies down the Ho Chi Minh trail increased steadily during the years of the heaviest bombing. The United States developed a variety of devices to detect infiltration. By 1968 American planes had dropped 20,000 electric sensors along the trail, which could pick up the sound, the smell, or the vibration of passing troops and trucks. But the sensors were not sensitive enough to tell the difference between an enemy soldier and anything else that might be passing nearby. A water buffalo unfortunate enough to wander by one of the "people-sniffer" sensors could find itself the target of tons of expensive American bombs (a single B-52 sortie cost American taxpayers $30,000 for the bombs alone). It was estimated that it took an average of 100 tons of bombs dropped along the Ho Chi Minh trail to kill a single North Vietnamese soldier.

So the United States controlled the air over Vietnam but paid a heavy price for it. American losses over North Vietnam alone, from 1965 through 1968, included 918 aircraft shot down and 818 crew members killed. All told, the United States lost 3,689 fixed-wing aircraft and 4,857 helicopters in the fighting in Indochina by the time the war ended. The United States had assembled a massive armada of sleek fighter-bombers, whirring helicopters, and deadly B-52s in and around Vietnam, but found it made little difference in the final outcome of the war. In *Dispatches,* his memoir of a year spent in Vietnam as a war correspondent, journalist Michael Herr managed to sum up in a single sentence the futility of all that technological know-how and expensive hardware: "Airmobility, dig it, you weren't going anywhere."

10
THE HOME FRONT

Debate and Protest

Vietnam was not the first U.S. war to stir dissent and protest at home. The War of 1812 was so unpopular in New England that several states in the region considered leaving the Union before the war was brought to its close. The 19th-century writer and naturalist Henry David Thoreau was so upset about the Mexican War that he refused to pay taxes even though it meant being sent to jail. During the Civil War, riots broke out in New York City in opposition to the North's military draft; the draft allowed those who could afford it to buy their way out of military service, leading some reluctant draftees to complain that this was a rich man's war and a poor man's fight. In April 1917, when President Woodrow Wilson asked Congress for a declaration of war against imperial Germany, many congressmen and senators voted against the resolution. Pacifists and socialists rallied popular support against the war until their leaders were rounded up and imprisoned under hastily passed laws forbidding such activities. World War II and the Korean War saw relatively little protest, though the American public was by no means enthusiastic about the inconclusive conflict in Korea.

The Vietnam War, America's longest war, also proved its most divisive. Between 1965 and 1973 the Vietnam issue dominated political debate in the country, destroying the presidency of Lyndon Johnson and ending the Democratic Party's long-standing dominance of the White House. (From 1932 through 1964 the Democrats won the presidency in six of the eight presidential elections held in those years; from 1968 through 1988 they lost five out of six presidential elections.)

While "hawks" (those who were prowar) and "doves" (those who were antiwar) debated in the halls of Congress, antiwar protesters took to the streets in the largest demonstrations ever staged over any issue in American history. Public support for the war eroded, and in time a majority came to view American involvement in Vietnam as a mistake.

The American media (newspapers, magazines, and television) reported on and reflected this division in the nation over the issue of the Vietnam War. Some military leaders believed the media was the *cause* of the division over the war. Among them was Adm. Harry D. Felt, who was in charge of the U.S. command in the Pacific in the early part of the war. When asked a critical question by a reporter at a Saigon press conference, Felt snapped back, "Why don't you get on the team?"

In fact, most reporters—particularly in the early years of the war— felt that they *were* on the "team." The overwhelming majority of American newspapers and newsmagazines editorially endorsed the war during most of the 1960s. Very few editors or reporters shared the view of I. F. Stone (an independent journalist who exposed contradictions in the official version of the Tonkin Gulf incident) that "every government is run by liars and nothing they say should be believed." Neil Sheehan, a reporter from United Press International who was stationed in South Vietnam during the early years of the war, would later write that during the cold war much of the reporting that appeared in U.S. papers "was weighted toward the furthering of the anti-Communist crusade." When the war in Vietnam began, American newspapers endorsed it without reservation. Young reporters like Sheehan and David Halberstam of the *New York Times* sometimes sent in critical reports from South Vietnam on the progress of pacification or the Diem government's handling of the Buddhist crisis. But they still believed in what the United States said it was trying to do in Vietnam. "The resident correspondents in Vietnam were . . . questioning detail, not substance," Sheehan wrote. "We thought it our duty to help win the war by reporting the truth of what was happening in order both to inform the public and to put the facts before those in power so that they could make correct decisions." Sheehan, Halberstam, and others had not yet "questioned the justice and good sense of U.S. intervention."

The quality of much of the reporting from Vietnam through the mid-1960s suffered from the media's willingness to believe what they were told by government and military officials. *Time* magazine's uncritical reporting of the Gulf of Tonkin "battle" in August 1964 was typical, full of colorful but imaginary detail:

> Through the darkness, from the west and south, the intruders boldly sped. There were at least six of them, Russian-designed "Swatow" gunboats armed with 37-mm. and 28-mm. guns, and P-4s. At 9:52 they opened fire on the destroyers with automatic weapons, this time from as close as 2,000 yards.

As the war dragged on, and statements by the military and other government leaders proved unfounded, some members of the press grew more suspicious of the official version. *New York Times* reporter Harrison Salisbury was the first American journalist to send back reports directly from North Vietnam. Until his trip to Hanoi in December 1966, no newspapers had questioned the administration's claims that civilian targets in North Vietnam were strictly off limits to American bombers. Salisbury, seeing the ruins in Hanoi and other cities with his own eyes, sent back a report that "United States planes are dropping an enormous weight of explosives on purely civilian targets." Some reporters began to refer to the daily press briefings by the Joint United States Public Affairs Office (JUSPAO), which handled the U.S. military's public relations in Saigon, as the "Five o'Clock Follies."

Television played a major role in shaping public perceptions of the war. Vietnam was, as has often been noted, America's first televised war. Almost every day during the war, combat footage shot only a few hours earlier appeared on the television screen at 6:30 P.M. in living rooms across America. The presence of television cameras could have strange effects on the men being filmed. Michael Herr, a print journalist, wrote in his memoir of Vietnam, *Dispatches:*

> You don't know what a media freak is until you've seen the way a few of those grunts would run around during a fight when they knew that there was a television crew nearby; they were actually making war movies in their heads.

Television reporting tended to focus on dramatic footage of combat, not on complicated questions of Vietnamese politics and history. Yet sometimes the images that appeared on the screen led viewers to wonder about the official justifications for the war. CBS correspondent

Morley Safer, for example, reported in August 1965 on a marine search-and-destroy operation in Cam Ne. The film he shot that day showed marines setting fire to the straw-roofed huts of peasants with their cigarette lighters, a questionable way of "winning the hearts and minds" of the Vietnamese people. As long as the war seemed to be going in America's favor, however, exposure to television coverage did not shake most viewers' faith in what the government told them. A *Newsweek* poll taken in 1967 showed that most Americans felt that television reporting made them more likely to support the war, suggesting that it was not the media's failure to "get on the team" that made the war in Vietnam go badly for the United States.

Despite the near unanimity with which the Tonkin Gulf Resolution passed both houses of Congress (with only Wayne Morse of Oregon and Ernest Gruening of Alaska voting in opposition), political debate over the war would soon rage furiously in Washington. Senator J. William Fulbright from Arkansas was a key figure in the emerging "dove" (antiwar) group in Congress. As chairman of the Senate Foreign Relations Committee, Fulbright was an influential leader in Washing-

Secretary of State Dean Rusk (left) in Washington, D.C., with Senator J. W. Fulbright, chairman of the Senate Foreign Relations Committee, May 31, 1961 *(National Archives)*

ton, which is why Lyndon Johnson had asked him personally to introduce the Gulf of Tonkin Resolution in Congress in 1964. Within a few months Fulbright had grown troubled over the direction of U.S. policy in South Vietnam. In televised hearings before the Senate Foreign Relations Committee in February 1966, he openly opposed administration policy in Vietnam. And in April, in a widely noted speech at Johns Hopkins University, Fulbright warned that the United States was displaying the same "arrogance of power" in Vietnam that had "destroyed great nations in the past."

In addition to Fulbright, Gruening, and Morse, Democratic senators Frank Church of Idaho, George McGovern of South Dakota, Gaylord Nelson of Wisconsin, Eugene McCarthy of Minnesota, Robert Kennedy of New York, and several others began to speak out against the war. Doves were unable to convince a majority in either the Senate or the House of Representatives to vote against administration policy. A resolution to repeal the Tonkin Gulf Resolution, introduced in the Senate in March 1966 by Wayne Morse, was defeated by a vote of 92 to 5. But antiwar members of Congress were able to use the debate in Washington to raise questions about U.S. goals and the conduct of the war in Vietnam. In February 1968 the Senate Foreign Relations Committee held hearings on the events four years earlier in the Tonkin Gulf. Secretary of Defense Robert McNamara admitted that the information he presented to Congress in 1964 on what went on in the Tonkin Gulf had been misleading. Such revelations contributed to the administration's "credibility gap." Lyndon Johnson hated his congressional critics, particularly Robert Kennedy, the younger brother of the late president. Johnson suspected Kennedy of wanting to replace him in the White House.

Although questions were raised in the media and Congress about the nature and direction of the war, the greatest opposition developed outside those institutions. The United States had never before seen an antiwar movement on the scale or the breadth of the one that grew up in opposition to the Vietnam War. There were many things about the war that disturbed protesters: the secrecy with which successive administrations had led the United States into involvement in Vietnam; the uncertainty of American war aims; the danger of involving China and the Soviet Union in a much wider war; the unpopular nature of the South Vietnamese government; the torture of Viet Cong prisoners; the mistreatment of civilians, including indiscriminate bombing in both

South and North Vietnam; and the use of such terrifying weapons as napalm bombs (napalm was a kind of flaming petroleum jelly that stuck to and melted human flesh on contact).

The 1960s began as an era of great idealism in the United States, particularly among the young. The decade opened with John Kennedy's inaugural address, which challenged Americans to "ask not what your country can do for you, but what you can do for your country." Young people on college campuses responded by joining the newly created Peace Corps or training for careers in public service. The campuses were expanding rapidly as millions of "baby boom" youngsters turned 18. (The baby boom was the popular term for the sharp jump in the U.S. birth rate that occurred after World War II.) Many college students felt that as a group they had the power and responsibility to make the world a better place. And, despite Kennedy's own hard-line foreign policies, many felt that it was time for the United States to put the cold war behind it. The emergence in the South of the black Civil Rights movement (which included among its leaders the Reverend Martin Luther King, Jr.) inspired many Americans, young and old, black and white. Social protest proved that it could deliver genuine social gains, like the Civil Rights Act of 1964 and the Voting Rights Act of 1965. Some future leaders of the antiwar movement, like Students for a Democratic Society (SDS) founder Tom Hayden, were drawn into political activism through the Civil Rights movement. Lyndon Johnson's "War on Poverty" programs also seemed part of the same trend toward a more just and equal society.

But the war in Vietnam threatened the gains being made by the civil rights movement and the War on Poverty. The war seemed to young idealists like a betrayal of the promise of John Kennedy's "New Frontier" and Lyndon Johnson's "Great Society." "What kind of America is it," SDS asked in its call for an April 1965 antiwar march in Washington, D.C., "whose response to poverty and oppression in South Vietnam is napalm and defoliation, whose response to poverty and oppression in Mississippi is . . . silence?"

Some 25,000 people turned out for the SDS march, a crowd that astonished the organizers. Smaller protests against U.S. policies in Vietnam had taken place over the past few years; the first known public demonstrations took place in August 1963 in New York and Philadelphia, in protest of the Diem regime's treatment of Buddhists. Within a few years, 25,000 would seem like a very small number; in April 1967,

Tom Hayden and the Battle of Good and Evil in the Streets of Chicago

LIKE MANY STUDENT ACTIVISTS IN THE 1960s, TOM Hayden had been deeply influenced by the southern Civil Rights movement. After graduating from the University of Michigan in the spring of 1961, Hayden went south as a volunteer in the movement. That fall, he was beaten by white segregationists in Mississippi. The next spring he authored the "Port Huron Statement," the founding document of Students for a Democratic Society (SDS), the principal organization of the New Left (and so named for the town in Michigan where SDS had its national convention in 1962). In the later 1960s Hayden was one of the leaders of the radical wing of the antiwar movement, arguing for a strategy of "bringing the war home" through disruptive street confrontations. Hayden put this strategy to the test in the demonstrations that he helped organize at the Chicago Democratic convention in August 1968, where protesters battled police for control of the streets. Such confrontational tactics proved politically self-defeating for the antiwar movement and a tragic outcome for the sense of moral urgency shared by so many young people in the 1960s.

300,000 turned out for an antiwar march in New York; in November 1969 a half-million marched in Washington. It was not just students who turned out; large numbers of older, middle-class adults were mobilized by groups like Women's Strike for Peace (WSP) and Clergy and Laity Concerned about Vietnam (CALCAV).

The war in Vietnam helped radicalize a generation of Americans. Many began their opposition to the war thinking that the war represented a mistake, but later came to believe that the war revealed fundamental flaws in American society. Reverend Martin Luther King, Jr., in a speech in a New York City church in April 1967, accused the United States government of being "the greatest purveyor [source] of violence in the world today." For King the Vietnam War was more than just an accident; it was a mirror of everything wrong in the United States. "If we are to get on the right side of the world revolution," King told his audience, "we as a nation must undergo a radical revolution of values."

Daniel and Philip Berrigan and Catholic Antiwar Resistance

THE ROMAN CATHOLIC CHURCH, A TRADITIONAL AND conservative institution, was in a state of great change in the 1960s. Under Pope John XXIII, the church reformed its liturgy, expanded ecumenical contacts, and began to emphasize a distinctly Catholic responsibility for social justice. In the United States, many priests and nuns were drawn to the Civil Rights movement. Daniel Berrigan, a Jesuit priest, and his brother Philip Berrigan, a Josephite father, played a leading role in what became known as the Catholic Resistance, a small group of religiously inspired antiwar activists who committed acts of civil disobedience to protest the war in Vietnam. In May 1968 the Berrigan brothers were part of a group of nine Catholic activists who broke into a draft board in Catonsville, Maryland, seized draft records, and burned them with a concoction of homemade napalm. Their actions, for which they were indicted and eventually imprisoned, led to a wave of similar acts of nonviolent destruction across the country (sometimes involving pouring human blood over the records). Many Catholics who might otherwise have had little sympathy for radical antiwar protesters, viewed the Berrigans as spiritual folk heroes.

The antiwar movement, drawing on the example of the Civil Rights movement, tried out many new protest tactics. For example, at the University of Michigan at Ann Arbor on March 24, 1965, the first "teach-ins" were held just three weeks after the marines landed at Danang. Three thousand students stayed up all night to listen to and participate in debate over the war. Dozens of other campuses organized teach-ins that spring. Over the next few years, several thousand young men of draft age either burned their draft cards or returned them to the Selective Service System; others simply declared their unwillingness to be drafted for the war in Vietnam, despite the heavy prison sentences such actions could bring; and several thousand young American men moved to Canada rather than run the risk of being drafted or jailed. Popular antidraft buttons included slogans like "Not with my life, you don't" and "Make love, not war." The young draft resisters were supported by some Americans past draft age, such as Dr. Benjamin Spock,

THE HOME FRONT

the famous pediatrician who was indicted in January 1968 for encouraging draft refusal.

Frustration over the war's escalation led to growing militancy on the part of many protesters. On college campuses students attempted to block recruiting by the military and corporations like Dow Chemical Company (a manufacturer of napalm). Some young protesters began to carry the red-and-blue flags of the Viet Cong to demonstrations, and a few burned American flags. Antiwar protesters were sometimes attacked by the police; some protesters fought back; a few actually initiated violence. On October 21, 1967, 50,000 protesters marched on the Pentagon, the headquarters of the U.S. Department of Defense, under a new slogan "from dissent to resistance." Several thousand slipped through the lines of military police who surrounded the

U.S. marshals bodily remove a protester during an outbreak of violence at the anti–Vietnam War demonstration at the Pentagon in Washington, D.C. *(National Archives)*

Pentagon to bring their nonviolent protest to the very steps of the "war machine."

Many older or more conservative Americans were convinced that the peace demonstrations were unpatriotic and possibly even traitorous. House minority leader (and future president) Gerald Ford of Michigan charged that the 1967 Pentagon protest had been organized in Hanoi. Lyndon Johnson was frequently a target of antiwar protesters, who chanted, "Hey, hey, LBJ, how many kids did you kill today?" Johnson authorized the Federal Bureau of Investigation (FBI) to probe, infiltrate, and disrupt antiwar organizing. He also ordered the CIA to look into the charges that the antiwar movement was controlled by foreign powers. There was no doubt that Hanoi welcomed the spread of antiwar sentiment in the United States, but the CIA reported that "we see no significant evidence that would prove Communist control or direction of the U.S. peace movement or its leaders."

Anti–Vietnam War demonstration: Members of the military police keep back protesters during sit-in at the Mall entrance to the Pentagon in Washington, D.C., October 21, 1967. *(U.S. Army)*

"Flower Power"

THE COUNTERCULTURE AND THE WAR

IT IS ONE OF THE MORE ENDURING CLICHÉS OF THE Vietnam War: a long-haired young man or woman in a shabby-chic hippie getup, placing a flower in the barrel of a weapon held by a soldier or National Guardsman at an antiwar demonstration. Like many clichés, it can conceal as much as it reveals, because antiwar protesters in the 1960s came in all kinds of garb, hairstyles, ages, and philosophies. At any fair-sized antiwar demonstration, plumbers, priests, military veterans, and even active duty GIs could be found in the ranks of protesters.

There were also, to be sure, many hippies. In his account of the October 1967 antiwar demonstration in Washington, D.C., novelist Norman Mailer wrote that many of those who marched on the Pentagon that day looked "like the legions of Sgt. Pepper's Band" (a reference to the Beatles album). The escalation of the war in Vietnam in the mid-1960s coincided with and also contributed to the growth of the counterculture. By the decade's end, as many as 3 million young Americans chose to identify themselves with alternative lifestyles—which could mean moving "back to the land" or to an urban commune, dropping out of "straight" occupations, and—frequently—smoking marijuana and ingesting hallucinogenic drugs.

"Make Love Not War" was a popular slogan among hippies and antiwar protesters alike. But what must be remembered is that just as not all antiwar protesters were hippies, so not all hippies protested against the war. Many of those drawn to the counterculture rejected all forms of political involvement, including protest politics. "Flower Power" could mean putting a daisy in a gun barrel; it could also mean cultivating one's own garden far away from the sound of angry protests.

In 1965 President Johnson's policies in Vietnam enjoyed overwhelming public support. That support eroded as years passed, American casualties mounted, and the long-promised victory still seemed as distant as ever. In October 1967, for the first time, public opinion polls revealed that a plurality (that is, a majority of those who expressed an opinion) agreed that it had been a mistake to send U.S. troops to fight in Vietnam. But it was a long time before most Americans were willing to admit defeat in Vietnam. It was not until 1971 that a majority of Americans polled favored "immediate withdrawal" from the conflict; others favored negotiations or some other compromise solution.

The most visible protesters were primarily middle class, many of them college students. But the polls revealed that working-class Americans were more likely than those from the middle and upper classes to oppose the war, because it was their children who were doing most of the fighting and dying. Many of those who came to oppose the war were not "antiwar" in any deep sense. Their feeling about the war was summed up in the often heard phrase that the United States should either "win or get out" of Vietnam. Most of those who came to oppose the war never took part in any demonstration against it. Even as the war came to be seen as unwinnable, antiwar protesters were still dismissed as unpatriotic.

By 1967 "dump Johnson" sentiment was growing among the liberal rank-and-file of the Democratic Party. Allard Lowenstein, a liberal activist previously involved in the Civil Rights movement, searched far and wide for a candidate who might be willing to challenge Johnson in the 1968 Democratic Party primaries. Most of those he approached, including Robert Kennedy, turned him down cold. It was considered impossible to deny an incumbent president the renomination of his own party. Finally, in October Senator Eugene McCarthy of Minnesota agreed to challenge Johnson on an antiwar platform. In the months that followed, Lowenstein was able to organize an impressive number of students to work for McCarthy's campaign in the upcoming primaries. The students promised to go "clean for Gene," cutting their hair and putting on their most respectable clothes to knock on doors on behalf of the peace candidate. No one who knew anything about the realities of American politics took McCarthy's chances in the primaries seriously. But that was before the Communists' Tet Offensive. Tet, the Vietnamese New Year celebration, proved to be the moment when the Vietnam War reached its decisive turning point. Lyndon Johnson's political career was one of Tet's many victims.

11

THE TET
OFFENSIVE

━◆┼∞───────────────────────────────

In November 1967 Gen. William Westmoreland made a brief trip from Vietnam to Washington, D.C. He was full of optimism about the war. Stepping off the plane, he told reporters: "I have never been more encouraged in the four years that I have been in Vietnam. We are making real progress." The next day he told reporters that the "phaseout" of U.S. involvement in Vietnam could begin within two years. And on November 21, in a speech before the National Press Club, Westmoreland assured the reporters and the American public that the "light at the end of the tunnel" in Vietnam had now become visible. Victory, he declared, "lies within our grasp."

Westmoreland's predictions would come back to haunt him during Vietnam's Tet holiday, at the end of January 1968. Tet, which marks the start of the lunar new year, is celebrated in Vietnam with feasts and fireworks. In past years, both sides in the war had observed cease-fires over the holiday. Half the South Vietnamese army and national police were on leave when Tet began on January 30, 1968. But on the Communist side, 70,000 Viet Cong and North Vietnamese soldiers were readying themselves for the supreme contest of the war.

The Communists had been preparing for this moment for months. In 1967 they launched a series of diversionary attacks on American bases in I Corps, the northern region of South Vietnam, to draw American attention and resources away from the more populated regions to the south. The marine base at Khe Sanh, located near the Laotian border and the Ho Chi Minh trail, and sitting astride an old French-built

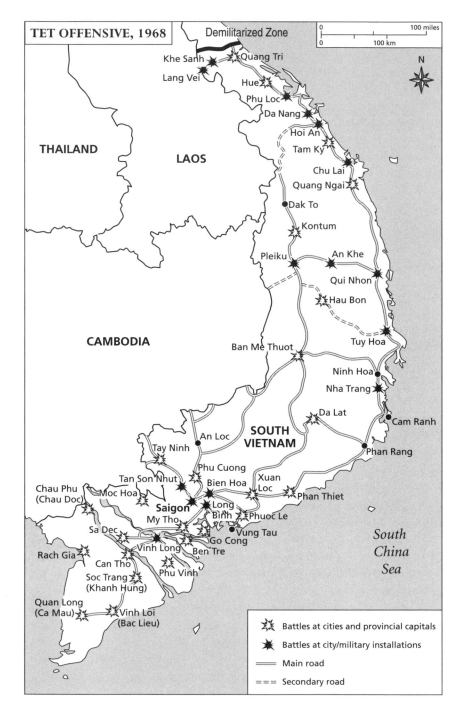

TET OFFENSIVE, 1968

Demilitarized Zone

Khe Sanh
Quang Tri
Lang Vei
Hue
Phu Loc
Da Nang
Hoi An
Tam Ky
Chu Lai
Quang Ngai
Dak To
Kontum
Pleiku
An Khe
Qui Nhon
Hau Bon
Ban Me Thuot
Tuy Hoa
Ninh Hoa
Nha Trang
Da Lat
Cam Ranh
An Loc
SOUTH
VIETNAM
Tay Ninh
Phan Rang
Phu Cuong
Tan Son Nhut
Bien Hoa
Xuan
Loc
Chau Phu
(Chau Doc)
Moc Hoa
Phan Thiet
Saigon
Long
Binh
Phuoc Le
My Tho
Sa Dec
Go Cong
Vung Tau
Rach Gia
Vinh Long
Ben Tre
Can Tho
Phu Vinh
Soc Trang
(Khanh Hung)
Quan Long
(Ca Mau)
Vinh Loi
(Bac Lieu)

THAILAND

LAOS

CAMBODIA

South
China
Sea

N

0   100 miles
0   100 km

Battles at cities and provincial capitals
Battles at city/military installations
Main road
Secondary road

road called Route 9, was surrounded by tens of thousands of North Vietnamese troops. Westmoreland was convinced that when the Communists launched their next offensive, overrunning Khe Sanh would be their major objective.

The Communists also smuggled men and weapons into and around South Vietnam's major cities and provincial capitals. "Mourners" carried coffins filled with weapons and ammunition and buried them at pagodas and churches where they could be easily dug up later. Explosives were concealed in baskets of tomatoes and rice. Viet Cong soldiers in civilian clothes mingled with crowds of South Vietnamese civilians returning to the cities for the Tet celebration. U.S. military intelligence analysts knew that the Communists were planning some kind of spectacular attack, but did not believe it would come during Tet, or that it would be nationwide. When some Communist units apparently jumped the gun and launched assaults in the early morning of January 30 on seven cities in northern South Vietnam, the American military command canceled a 36-hour cease-fire that had been set for the Tet holiday. American units were put on alert. But since they had been on alert many times before, most Americans were not prepared for the storm that was about to break upon them.

The Tet Offensive began shortly before 3 A.M. on the morning of January 31. One of the most spectacular attacks was launched against the U.S. embassy in Saigon. The embassy, the symbol of the American presence in South Vietnam, was at the center of a fortified compound that covered four acres. A Viet Cong suicide squad of 19 men blasted a three-foot hole through the compound's outer walls with an explosive charge, then gunned down the guards who tried to stop them from entering the compound. Once inside, the Viet Cong fought a six-hour-long battle with marine guards and military police who rushed to reinforce them. Five Americans were killed. Although the Viet Cong never made it inside the main embassy building, it was left pockmarked by rocket and machine-gun fire. The Great Seal of the United States, which had hung over its front door, was blasted by enemy fire and fell to the ground. Although all of the invaders were killed or captured, they had proven that there was no place in Vietnam that was secure from attack.

Meanwhile, it seemed as if all of South Vietnam was about to fall to the Communists, who attacked more than 100 cities, towns, and military bases. Communist troops captured Hue, Dalat, Kontum, and Quang Tri. Four thousand Communist troops attacked a number of

Armored personnel carriers move into position against Tet Offensive, February 1, 1968. *(National Archives)*

targets in Saigon. Tan Son Nhut air base, where American military headquarters were located, was hit by shelling and ground attack. Viet Cong suicide squads attacked the presidential palace and captured the main government radio station, where they held out for six hours before the building was recaptured. Heavy fighting lasted for days in the Cholon district of Saigon. From the roof of the Caravelle Hotel in central Saigon, war correspondents watched the battle every night after dinner; the scene was illuminated by the fires in Cholon and tracer bullets fired by American gunships hovering over enemy positions.

On February 1, early in the fight for Saigon, a Viet Cong soldier in civilian clothes was captured by South Vietnamese police and dragged before Gen. Nguyen Ngoc Loan, chief of the national police force. The general put a revolver to the man's head and fired. The entire episode, including the man falling to the street with blood spurting from his head, was photographed and filmed by an Associated Press photographer and an NBC television cameraman. The next morning the photograph of the execution dominated the front page of American newspapers; that evening the scene was broadcast on NBC television news. Many Americans were horrified. Secretary of State Dean Rusk was furious after watching the NBC news broadcast. "Whose side are you on?" he demanded of the newsmen a few days later. Why could they not find "constructive" stories to report from Vietnam, instead of "probing for the things that one can bitch about," like the Saigon execution?

Day after day and week after week, the Tet Offensive continued to dominate the headlines. The U.S. and South Vietnamese military had to fight city by city to dislodge the enemy. The United States used its heavy firepower to full effect, blasting the Viet Cong out of the towns it controlled. In the Mekong Delta, after the enemy was driven from the ruins of what had been the city of Ben Tre, a U.S. Army major told a reporter, "It became necessary to destroy the town to save it." Along with Westmoreland's "light at the end of the tunnel," that turned out to be one of the war's best-remembered phrases.

Some of the fiercest fighting of the Tet Offensive, and the war, took place in the battle to recapture the old imperial city of Hue, which until 1968 was the most beautiful city in South Vietnam. Two regiments of North Vietnamese soldiers infiltrated the city before Tet; with support from other North Vietnamese forces stationed outside, they seized control on January 31. They took up strong defensive positions within the Citadel, the old city of Hue that was surrounded by stone walls and

Bodies of enemy soldiers lie in the road at Long Binh as Tet Offensive combat rages on, February 1, 1968. *(National Archives)*

moats. U.S. Marines and Army Air Cavalry forces arrived over the next few days to retake the city; along with their South Vietnamese allies they fought a bitter, house-to-house battle that lasted 25 days in the cold, heavy rains of the monsoon season. Sometimes the two sides were only 20 or 30 yards apart, firing at each other from apartment windows or behind piles of rubble. Heavy artillery and air strikes helped the marines kill nearly 5,000 of the Communist soldiers, as well as many of Hue's civilians. On February 24, South Vietnamese troops ripped down the Viet Cong flag from the south wall of the Citadel, where it had flown since January 31.

Like Ben Tre, Hue was virtually destroyed in the fighting. Further horrors were discovered after the battle was finished. Mass graves were uncovered containing the bodies of 2,800 South Vietnamese civilians executed by the Communists in the early days of the battle, the worst Communist atrocity of the war. Several American and European civilians captured in the city were also executed. After Hue was recaptured, South Vietnamese assassination squads killed some of the city's residents who had reportedly aided the Communists when they controlled the city.

On the morning that the Tet Offensive was launched, General Westmoreland remained convinced that the enemy's real goal was the conquest of the marine base at Khe Sanh. The attack on Saigon and other cities, he declared, "is a diversionary effort to take the attention away from the northern part of the country." Some military men thought that the exact opposite was the case; it was the attack on Khe Sanh that was the "diversionary effort." Most historians agree. But the United States had good reason to be concerned about the defenders of Khe Sanh, who had been heavily shelled since January 21, 10 days before the start of the Tet Offensive. The 6,000 marines and South Vietnamese soldiers at the base were surrounded and cut off by 15,000 to 20,000 North Vietnamese regulars. They could be resupplied only by air. With heavy clouds and deep jungle covering the rugged hillsides of the area, the Communists encircling the base were invisible from the air. To many observers, the siege of Khe Sanh was all too reminiscent of the battle of Dien Bien Phu in 1954, where the surrender of the French garrison marked the triumph of the Communist-led anticolonial struggle. One of the units surrounding Khe Sanh, the North Vietnamese 304th Division, had taken part in the siege of Dien Bien Phu. And at one point during the assault, General Giap himself, the Communist commander at Dien Bien Phu, came down to Khe Sanh for a firsthand look.

Diversion or not, the siege of Khe Sanh continued as the Tet Offensive wound down elsewhere. "I don't want any damn Dinbinphoo," Lyndon Johnson told the Joint Chiefs of Staff, making them sign a document promising that the base could be held. The marines holding Khe Sanh were not sure they could hold out against the expected massive assault of North Vietnamese troops. A nearby Special Forces camp at Langvei was overrun in early February by North Vietnamese troops using tanks; this marked the first time tanks had been used by the Communists in South Vietnam. Every day the marines were pounded by Communist artillery, and every night they remained on alert for Communist probing attacks. Their casualties were heavy. Kevin Macaulay, a corporal with the Third Marine Division, wrote his parents from Khe Sanh in late January:

My morale is not the best because my best buddy was killed the day before yesterday. I was standing about 20 feet from him and a 60-mm mortar exploded next to him. He caught a piece of shrapnel in the head. I carried him over to the aid station where he died. I cried my eyes out. I have seen death before but nothing as close as this . . . Two days before that four other Marines in my company were killed by a rocket exploding on the floor of their bunker. They were killed instantly but their bodies were horribly mangled. I think with all the death and destruction I have seen in the past week I have aged greatly. I feel like an old man now.

The United States responded with air attacks, including B-52 raids on suspected Communist troop concentrations around the base. All told, the surrounding countryside was plastered with more than 100,000 tons of bombs during the siege, killing thousands of Communist soldiers. Finally on April 1, the First Air Cavalry began Operation Pegasus, the relief of Khe Sanh. They pushed their way westward along Communist-controlled Route 9 until they reached Khe Sanh on April 6. More than 200 marines were killed at Khe Sanh and 1,600 wounded. Then, after all the bloodshed, the base was quietly abandoned by the Americans in June.

No one won the Tet Offensive. More than 1,100 Americans were killed in the first two weeks of Tet, along with several thousand South Vietnamese. The United States claimed that more than 30,000 Communists were killed in the same period. General Westmoreland argued

In Saigon, black smoke rises from fires set during the attacks of the Tet Offensive in 1968. *(National Archives)*

that Tet was a military disaster for the Communists. The "general uprising" that they had called for among the South Vietnamese population failed to take place. Their casualties were much higher than those of the Americans and South Vietnamese. The native-born southerners in the Viet Cong were particularly hard hit, and for the rest of the war North Vietnamese regulars did most of the fighting in the south.

THE TET OFFENSIVE

After the war it was revealed that the North Vietnamese military leaders themselves regarded the Tet Offensive as something of a military failure. But the Americans were not the victors of Tet. Even though the called-for uprising did not occur, the Communists had demonstrated that they were not just foreign invaders, but enjoyed considerable support in the south. Otherwise it would not have been possible for them to smuggle thousands of men and tons of weapons and ammunition into South Vietnamese cities without ever being betrayed to the American or South Vietnamese intelligence agencies. The pacification program, never very successful, was wrecked in much of the South Vietnamese countryside as a result of Tet; the U.S. command in Saigon estimated that the South Vietnamese government lost control over more than 1 million people after Tet. And although the Communists paid a great price for their offensive, they were still able to keep up their pressure on the Americans in the months that followed. In May they launched another offensive, referred to as a "mini-Tet," with attacks on more than 100 cities and bases, including Saigon. The United States lost 562 dead in the week ending May 11, the highest weekly total of the war, and lost nearly 2,000 dead during that month, the highest monthly total.

The Communists' greatest success with the Tet Offensive was the psychological victory they scored in the United States. After Tet, it was impossible for Americans to believe the reassuring promises of General Westmoreland and President Johnson that victory was around the corner. Walter Cronkite, anchorman of the CBS TV evening news and perhaps the most trusted newsman in the nation, was in the CBS newsroom when news of the Tet Offensive arrived. "What the hell is going on?" he exclaimed. "I thought we were winning the war!" Cronkite flew to South Vietnam in mid-February, and visited Hue while the battle still raged. In a special half-hour report broadcast after his return to the United States in late February, Cronkite declared:

> It seems now more certain than ever that the bloody experience of Vietnam is to end in a stalemate . . . It is increasingly clear to this reporter that the only rational way out then will be to negotiate, not as victors but as an honorable people who lived up to their pledge to defend democracy, and did the best they could.

When news leaked out in early March that General Westmoreland was requesting an additional 206,000 troops be sent to Vietnam, it added to the fears of Americans that the war was becoming a quagmire. Westmoreland was now so distrusted by the American public that the administration arranged to have him "kicked upstairs," appointing him army chief of staff in June 1968, to be replaced by his deputy, Gen. Creighton Abrams.

Another major victim of the Tet Offensive was Lyndon Johnson's political career. Senator Eugene McCarthy, who had announced his decision the previous fall to challenge the president in the 1968 primaries, charged after Tet that "the Administration's reports of progress [in Vietnam] are the products of their own self-deception." McCarthy astonished the nation by coming close to defeating Johnson in the New Hampshire primary on March 12. Not everyone who voted for McCarthy did so because they opposed the war; some wanted to register a protest against Johnson's apparent failure to win in Vietnam. But the vote revealed Johnson's political vulnerability. Four days later a much stronger candidate, Robert Kennedy, announced his decision to enter the race. Kennedy, like McCarthy, made opposition to the war the central issue of his campaign. By late March only

Walter Cronkite and a CBS camera crew use a jeep for a dolly while interviewing a commanding officer during the Battle of Hue City, February 20, 1968. *(National Archives)*

26 percent of the American public approved Johnson's handling of the war.

Johnson could not depend upon even his closest advisers to back his conduct of the war. Secretary of Defense Robert McNamara had already privately turned against the war and left the administration in January 1968. Clark Clifford replaced him. In February Johnson asked Clifford to assemble a task force within the Defense Department to study the military's request for more troops in Vietnam. Clifford had been a strong supporter of Johnson and the war for many years, but he now developed doubts very similar to those that had led McNamara to resign. As he told an interviewer years later:

> After a month in the Pentagon, I knew that we were wrong, and I knew that it wasn't really Communist aggression. What we were dealing with was a civil war in Vietnam. And I knew we had an absolute loser on our hands. We weren't ever going to win that war.

Clifford's task force report did not openly challenge continued U.S. involvement in Vietnam. But it did warn against committing additional troops to the fight and suggested a more cautious military strategy in Vietnam than the search-and-destroy operations that Westmoreland favored. Johnson, disturbed by the pessimism underlying the report, called for a meeting of a small group of senior advisers he referred to as the "Wise Men"—former cabinet officers, military men, and others who had advised him on other occasions. The Wise Men included former secretary of state Dean Acheson, former ambassador Henry Cabot Lodge, former national security adviser McGeorge Bundy, and retired generals Matthew Ridgway and Maxwell Taylor. Two members of Johnson's cabinet, Secretary of State Rusk and Secretary of Defense Clifford, attended the sessions in late March. The Wise Men were briefed by military and CIA officials, who told them that even with reinforcements it might take the United States another five to 10 years to defeat the Communists in Vietnam. At the end of two days of meetings, the Wise Men met with the president and delivered their verdict: The war was unwinnable with the present policies. Though there was some disagreement among them, the consensus of the Wise Men was that no additional troops should be sent to Vietnam, the bombing of North Vietnam should be halted, and the United States should move toward a negotiated settlement.

Johnson was shocked by this shift in opinion among these solidly anticommunist elder statesmen, some of whom had helped shape the policies that had gotten the United States involved in Vietnam in the first place. Although the antiwar movement had not been able to change Lyndon Johnson's policies directly, it had an effect on the Wise Men, and they in turn pushed Johnson in a new direction. As Johnson noted in his memoirs, the Wise Men "expressed deep concern about the divisions in our country. Some of them felt that those divisions were growing rapidly and might soon force withdrawal from Vietnam."

On Sunday March 31, Johnson spoke to the nation in a televised broadcast. That night he announced that the Communists' Tet Offensive had been a failure, but he did not offer any optimistic prediction of a "light at the end of the tunnel" in Vietnam. Instead he announced a halt to bombing raids in North Vietnam except for an area north of the DMZ. He called upon North Vietnamese leaders to join the United States in peace talks. And at the end, he astonished his listeners by declaring, "I shall not seek, and I will not accept, the nomination of my party for another term as your president." The Vietnam War had destroyed Johnson's presidency.

Three days after Johnson's speech, North Vietnamese leaders announced their willingness to take part in peace negotiations. American and North Vietnamese diplomats began meeting a few weeks later in Paris to discuss how the talks would be arranged. It turned out to be a long discussion, since the United States initially objected to the participation of the Viet Cong in peace talks, and the Communists objected to the participation of the Saigon government. Finally on November 1, Johnson halted all bombing over North Vietnam. (U.S. planes had continued since March to pound targets up to 225 miles north of the DMZ.) President Thieu of South Vietnam was still objecting to peace negotiations, but his goal was to delay any talks until after (he hoped) Richard Nixon's election to the presidency. All the while the year's death toll in Vietnam continued to mount. American losses in the war by the end of 1968 stood at 30,610 killed. Of these, 14,589, nearly half the total number, had been killed in the past year.

Richard Nixon received the Republican nomination for the presidency, implying he had a "secret plan" to end the war in Vietnam if elected. Meanwhile the Democratic Party splintered over the war issue. Eugene McCarthy and Robert Kennedy won most of the primaries in

1968

HOW THE WAR
WRECKED THE DEMOCRATIC PARTY

LYNDON JOHNSON GOT AWAY WITH RUNNING AS both the "war" candidate and the "peace" candidate in 1964. No Democratic candidate for president was going to get away with that kind of balancing act in the bitter 1968 presidential race. Eugene McCarthy and Robert Kennedy staked out positions in the Democratic primaries as antiwar candidates; it was left to Vice President Hubert Humphrey to defend the Johnson administration's conduct of the Vietnam War.

Despite the string of primary victories the two antiwar candidates had racked up in the spring, Humphrey's nomination at the Chicago Democratic convention in August was never seriously in doubt. Lyndon Johnson used all his influence to make sure that Humphrey continued to toe his administration's line on the war at the convention, and—although it took a divisive floor fight—he also made sure that the convention delegates did not adopt a minority-sponsored antiwar resolution.

Humphrey had been critical of Johnson's decision to escalate the war in 1965, although he had publicly supported the administration's policies. After his nomination, some advisers urged him to reach out to the party's antiwar wing to unite the Democrats against Republican nominee Richard Nixon. Trailing badly in the polls, Humphrey finally pledged in late September that, as president, he would halt the bombing of North Vietnam and "seek peace in every way possible." His show of independence from Johnson helped him gain ground against Nixon but lost him support in the White House. An embittered Johnson sat out most of the campaign, throwing active support to Humphrey only in the last few weeks before the election. In the three-way race for the presidency, Humphrey wound up losing to Nixon by less than one-tenth of 1 percent of the popular vote.

the spring, but Kennedy was assassinated in early June after winning the California primary. Vice President Hubert Humphrey entered the race for the presidency in April with President Johnson's support. In August, he won the Democratic Party's nomination at its chaotic National Convention in Chicago, which was marred by bloody street battles between antiwar protesters and Chicago police. Humphrey was too closely identified with Lyndon Johnson's failed policies in Vietnam to unite his party in the remaining weeks before the November election. On November 5, 1968, Richard Nixon was elected president of the United States, and on January 20, 1969, he was inaugurated. It was now Nixon's war.

12

NIXON'S WAR

1969–1973

The Democrats were out of the White House and the Republicans were back in. The war continued. Richard Nixon was the fifth American president in a quarter-century to face the question of what role the United States should play in Vietnam. He owed his election in 1968 in large measure to the American public's disgust with the failure of President Johnson's policies in Vietnam, but it was not clear exactly what the voters expected him to do. Although the polls revealed that most Americans viewed the initial U.S. involvement in Vietnam as a mistake, they were not yet willing to admit defeat at the hands of the Communists by supporting the immediate and total withdrawal of all U.S. troops from Vietnam. Not until 1971 would that position finally win majority support.

Some of Nixon's cabinet officers, like the new secretary of defense, Melvin Laird, believed that the American public was "fed up with the war" and that it was time to pull out of Vietnam. Nixon's national security adviser (later secretary of state), Henry Kissinger, thought that the best Americans could gain for the South Vietnamese government was a "decent interval" between the withdrawal of U.S. troops and the final Communist triumph. Nixon, however, believed that an American victory in Vietnam was still possible. A man who was shrewd, secretive, competitive, and personally insecure, Richard Nixon wanted to triumph where Democrats like John Kennedy and Lyndon Johnson had failed before him. At the same time he realized that he could not seem to be expanding or even continuing the war at present levels if he hoped to retain the support of the American public. He sought a way to continue to wage war while reducing U.S. troop and casualty levels in Vietnam.

Although President Johnson had turned down General Westmoreland's request for an additional 200,000 troops in the spring of 1968, the number of American servicemen continued to increase through the following year, peaking at 543,000 shortly after Richard Nixon took office in 1969. Over the next four years the bulk of American troops were withdrawn from Vietnam, but the war continued with even greater ferocity than before. What changed was the nationality of the corpses, in a process that Defense Secretary Laird dubbed "Vietnamization."

Vietnamization consisted of the gradual withdrawal of U.S. troops and the expansion and re-equipment of the South Vietnamese military, combined with intense American bombing. The South Vietnamese armed forces were built up into what was, at least on paper, a formidable fighting force of more than 1 million men, with 3 million more in local militia. Under Vietnamization, the ARVN was expected to carry the burden of the ground war (where most of the casualties were suffered), while American pilots continued to dominate the skies over South and North Vietnam. Laos, and (for the first time) Cambodia. Meanwhile, through Operation Phoenix, the CIA coordinated efforts to destroy the Viet Cong's political influence in the countryside through the arrest or assassination of key Communist activists. An estimated 20,000 were assassinated between 1968 and 1971.

In his 1985 book *No More Vietnams* (which, despite the title, argues that under his presidency the war in Vietnam was being won by the United States), Nixon conceded that antiwar sentiment had forced him to adopt the strategy of "Vietnamization":

> I doubt that we could have continued fighting the war if we had not been gradually withdrawing our troops. Since 1969, we had been faced with the danger of Congress legislating an end to our involvement. Anti-war senators and congressmen had been introducing resolutions to force us to trade a total withdrawal of our troops for the return of our POWs . . . We were able to prevent the passage of these bills only because our withdrawal announcements provided those whose support for the war was wavering with tangible evidence that our involvement was winding down.

Many were willing to accept Nixon's assurances that the war was coming to an end. After the exhausting crisis-ridden year of 1968, Americans were tired of hearing bad news from Vietnam and wanted to think about something else for a change. Newspapers and particularly television network news (under attack by Vice President Spiro Agnew and others for what they charged was liberal bias) began to downplay reporting on Americans in combat.

But if Americans at home were encouraged to forget about the war for weeks at a time, that did not mean that Nixon was any less devoted to defeating the Communists in Vietnam than Lyndon Johnson had been. In fact, Nixon hoped that his own reputation as a hard-line anti-communist would persuade the North Vietnamese to come to terms with the Americans. As he explained to White House aide H. R. ("Bob") Haldeman, shortly after taking office:

> I call it the Madman Theory, Bob. I want the North Vietnamese to believe that I've reached the point where I might do anything to stop the war. We'll just slip the word to them that, "for God's sake, you know Nixon is obsessed about Communists. We can't restrain him, when he's angry—and he has his hand on the nuclear button"—and Ho Chi Minh himself will be in Paris in two days begging for peace.

At the same time, Nixon was reaching out to Communist China and the Soviet Union, offering diplomatic recognition to the Chinese and trade deals to the Soviets. Nixon hoped that they would pressure their North Vietnamese allies to make concessions at the bargaining table, as they had done once before, in the 1954 Geneva negotiations.

While Nixon shaped his military and diplomatic strategy in the early months of his administration, heavy fighting continued in Vietnam. In another Communist "mini-Tet" in the first three weeks of February 1969, the United States lost more than 1,100 men killed. Another battle later that spring became a symbol of the futility of the ground war in Vietnam. In May 1969 a combined assault by the marines and troops from the 101st Airborne Division on Hill 937 in the A Shau Valley ran into stubborn North Vietnamese resistance. It took 11 attacks in 10 days to drive the Communists off the hill. The troops called the battle a "meat grinder," because it produced so many bloody bodies: 56 Americans were killed and 420 wounded in taking what became known as "Hamburger Hill." And, just as had happened at Khe Sanh, when the battle was over all the Americans were left with was another useless piece of real estate. Hamburger Hill was abandoned soon after its capture and reoccupied by the North Vietnamese.

The frustrations of fighting this kind of war led some American servicemen to seek revenge against ordinary Vietnamese civilians. The most infamous atrocity of the war took place in a little village known as My Lai 4 in Quang Ngai province in March 1968. The U.S. Army covered up the story of the My Lai massacre until it was revealed by Seymour Hersh, an investigative reporter, in the fall of 1969. The My Lai story shocked Americans, though many refused to believe, even in the face of overwhelming evidence, that American soldiers could have been guilty of war crimes.

On March 15, 1968, 80 men from Charlie Company of the First Battalion, Twentieth Infantry Brigade, under the command of Lt. William Calley were sent into My Lai to search for Viet Cong suspects. Over the past two months, nearly one-third of Charlie Company had been killed or wounded by booby traps, mines, and snipers. They blamed the local people for aiding the enemy. The Americans met no resistance at all that day in My Lai, but Calley ordered all the people in the village rounded up and killed. Calley personally murdered dozens of villagers. All told, more than 400 civilians, including old people, women, children, and babies were gunned down; at least one young woman was raped before she was killed. Some soldiers refused to join in the killing, despite Calley's threats to court-martial them. Hugh Thompson, an army warrant officer, witnessed the massacre from his helicopter. When he landed to evacuate some wounded civilians, he told his helicopter crew to fire on any soldier who tried to kill more civilians. Thompson managed to rescue nine civilians, five of them children. One wounded child died on the way to the hospital. Although Thompson reported to Calley's brigade commander what happened in My Lai, the army took no action against the men of Charlie Company. Instead, the civilian dead in My Lai were added to the enemy "body count"; *Stars and Stripes,* the army newspaper, reported that 128 Communist soldiers were killed in My Lai in "a day-long battle." General Westmoreland sent Charlie Company a personal message congratulating them for "outstanding action."

The army quietly decided to court-martial Calley a year later, after a Vietnam veteran named Ron Ridenhour (who had been in My Lai shortly after the massacre and heard accounts from friends who had taken part in the massacre) contacted dozens of government officials to get them to look into what happened in the village. Seymour Hersh learned of the court-martial and broke the story to the public. Calley was found guilty at his court-martial at Fort Benning, Georgia, on March 29, 1971, of the murder of 22 Vietnamese civilians. He was initially sentenced to life imprisonment at hard labor, but President Nixon reduced his sentence and allowed him to serve it in his own apartment under house arrest. In September 1975 Calley was released on parole.

In March 1969 Nixon began to try out his "madman theory." He ordered the launching of Operation Menu, a secret bombing campaign against the border regions of Cambodia where the North Vietnamese often took sanctuary. The bombing continued for the next 14 months. Nixon intended the bombings as a signal to North Vietnam that he was capable of tough, unpredictable measures. The American public and even much of the military command was kept in ignorance about Operation Menu; information about bombing missions was falsified to help keep it a secret. When a story about the bombing was leaked to the *New York Times* in May 1969, it did not attract much attention. Nixon, however, responded by ordering illegal wiretaps of government officials so that he could learn the source of the "leak." Some historians have argued that this decision marked the first step leading toward the Watergate domestic spying scandal that would destroy Nixon's presidency in 1974.

Nixon had secretly warned Hanoi that if no diplomatic concessions were made by November 1, he would use "measures of great consequence and force" against them. Ho Chi Minh had died on September 3, 1969, at the age of 79, but his successors showed no signs of changing their commitment to winning the war against the Americans. Nixon apparently backed down from whatever "measures" he had in mind when confronted with massive antiwar protests in the fall of 1969. More than 1 million people participated nationwide in an October 15 moratorium against the war, while a November 15 antiwar march in Washington brought a half-million protesters to the city. Nixon sought to discredit the antiwar movement by appealing to what he described as the "silent majority" of his supporters. "North Vietnam cannot defeat or humiliate the United States," he declared. "Only Americans can do that."

But Nixon understood that he enjoyed the support of his "silent majority" only so long as the war seemed to be winding down, which is why he kept announcing new troop withdrawals: 65,500 in 1969,

140,000 in 1970, 160,000 in 1971, and 157,000 in 1972. U.S. casualties dropped proportionately: 9,414 Americans died in Vietnam in 1969, 4,204 in 1970, 1,386 in 1971, and 300 in 1972. Nixon forgot that lesson only once, in the spring of 1970, when—acting impulsively—he ordered U.S. soldiers to cross the border into Cambodia. Most of Nixon's cabinet opposed the move. Henry Kissinger was one of the few important figures in the administration to back the president enthusiastically; he was rewarded with increased power in shaping Nixon's foreign policy.

Cambodia's ruler, Prince Norodom Sihanouk, had tried to keep his country neutral in the war by appeasing both sides. He had allowed the Communists to use his border regions as sanctuaries without protest, but he had also allowed the Americans to bomb his territory without protest. But in March 1970 Sihanouk's defense minister, Gen. Lon Nol, took power while Sihanouk was out of the country, and swung Cambodia behind the U.S. war effort. Nixon decided the moment had arrived to eliminate the Communist border sanctuaries once and for all. On April 29 a force of 32,000 U.S. soldiers and 48,000 ARVN soldiers launched what the White House referred to as an "incursion" (avoiding the use of the more politically charged term *invasion*) into Cambodian territory. President Nixon went on television the evening of April 30 to announce the action, declaring that if successful, it would eliminate the "headquarters for the entire communist military operation in South Vietnam." American credibility, he argued, was on the line:

> If, when the chips are down, the world's most powerful nation, the United States of America, acts like a pitiful, helpless giant, the forces of totalitarianism and anarchy will threaten free nations and free institutions throughout the world.

The war was back in the headlines. Antiwar members of Congress rushed to introduce new legislation that would require withdrawal from Indochina. The Tonkin Gulf Resolution was finally repealed. The Senate passed a bill prohibiting the use of U.S. troops in Cambodia within six weeks. But the strongest reaction came on the nation's college campuses. On May 1 Nixon had denounced students who protested against his policies as "these bums, you know, blowin' up the campuses." Some argued that Nixon's comments inflamed an already tense situation. Three days later, on May 4, Ohio National

Soldiers guard medical supplies, including penicillin, bandages, vitamins, and antimalaria pills, captured in Cambodia, 1970. *(National Archives)*

Guardsmen fired into a crowd of antiwar demonstrators on the campus of Kent State University, killing four. The combination of the invasion of Cambodia and the deaths at Kent State set off a national student strike. More than 400 colleges and universities were shut down and millions of students protested the war. Most of these protests were peaceful, although 30 campus Reserve Officer Training Corps (ROTC) buildings were burned down nationwide. One hundred thousand protesters converged on Washington on May 9 in a hastily arranged demonstration.

Nixon had his supporters too, including "hard hats" from New York City's construction trades who marched through the streets of the city to back U.S. policies in Indochina. But in the face of massive protests, Nixon again backed down, announcing that the Cambodia "incursion" would be over in a few weeks and that American troops would go no farther than 21 miles across the border. In the end, little was accomplished by the invasion. The Communist "headquarters," if it existed, was never found. The most lasting effect of the spring's events was to draw Cambodia into a war that Sihanouk had successfully kept it out

Kent State and the Fate
of the Antiwar Movement

IN *VIETNAM: THE WAR AT HOME,* A HISTORY OF THE antiwar movement published in 1973, journalist Thomas Powers noted that the "violence in Vietnam" seemed to encourage "a similar air of violence in the United States" in the late 1960s. The war, he wrote, contributed to "an appetite for extremes: people felt that history was accelerating, time was running out, great issues were reaching a point of final decision."

That "appetite for extremes" was much in evidence in the spring of 1970. By then students had been demonstrating against the war for five years. The early days of peaceful antiwar protest, involving such tactics as electoral referendums, vigils, and teach-ins, had increasingly given way in the later 1960s to sit-ins and building occupations, often ending in violent confrontations with the authorities. Some campus activists decided that the only way they could affect U.S. policy in Southeast Asia was by "bringing the war home" through disruptive tactics designed to make the political cost of continuing the conflict unacceptable.

The killings at Kent State University in Ohio, and the mass protests that followed, came close to realizing this vision of a war at home, at least on many college and university campuses. The protests actually succeeded in forcing the Nixon administration to curtail the invasion of Cambodia. But the war in Vietnam went on. And for the antiwar movement, partial victory seemed like no victory at all. When students returned to campuses in the fall of 1970, the antiwar movement had lost a great deal of its momentum. Four dead in Ohio, dozens of ROTC buildings burned to the ground, and hundreds arrested—yet nothing seemed to have changed. Revolutionary illusions were punctured and even the moderate majority of the antiwar movement seemed to lose heart.

of. Five years later the Khmer Rouge (Cambodian Communists) overthrew the Lon Nol government, installing a repressive regime that in a few years killed millions of Cambodians.

In February 1971 Nixon again decided to launch an invasion, this time into Laos, in an attempt to block traffic on the Ho Chi Minh trail. To avoid setting off another massive protest in the United States, only ARVN troops were used; they were carried into battle on American helicopters. The Laotian invasion was a key test of how well Vietnamization was proceeding, and it failed miserably. North Vietnam had been tipped off by its spies beforehand and laid a trap for the ARVN soldiers. Nearly 10,000 of the South Vietnamese troops were killed or wounded in the invasion. Others broke and ran. Some clung to the skids of departing helicopters, desperate to flee the battlefield.

The problem with the ARVN was not one of equipment or training, as most U.S. military advisers assumed. Rather, there was no government in Saigon able to inspire its men to stand and fight and die the way that the Viet Cong and North Vietnamese had shown they were willing to. The military regime of Nguyen Cao Ky and Nguyen Van Thieu had held elections, at the urging of the Americans, in 1967. Ky was elected vice president and Thieu president of the new civilian government. But it was not a free election; the only opposition candidate to run on an antiwar platform was arrested soon afterward by the government. In 1971 Thieu staged another election, this time running without opposition; he had a special law passed by the South Vietnamese legislature to keep Ky from running against him. Whether established by means of coups or voting, whether civilian or military, the Saigon government remained corrupt, inefficient, and unpopular throughout the war.

The morale of American soldiers fell drastically in the last years of the war. The military was plagued by desertions, drug abuse (marijuana, opium, and heroin were cheap and readily available in Vietnam), racial tension, and assaults on officers. (Such assaults were called "fragging" because they sometimes took the form of tossing a fragmentation grenade into an unpopular officer's tent; army records showed 551 "fraggings" between 1969 and 1972.) Some units even refused orders from their officers to go on patrol or into combat when they felt that the danger was too great; the elite Air Cav alone recorded 35 instances of men refusing to fight in 1970. In an article in the *Armed Forces Journal* in 1971, marine colonel Robert Heinl wrote that:

> The morale, discipline and battleworthiness of the U.S. Armed Forces are . . . lower and worse than at any time in this century and possibly in the history of the United States . . . Our army that now remains in Vietnam is in a state approaching collapse.

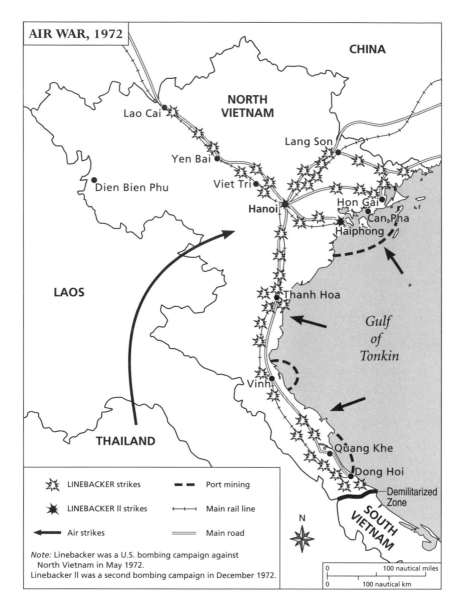

AIR WAR, 1972

CHINA

NORTH VIETNAM

Lao Cai

Lang Son

Yen Bai

Dien Bien Phu

Viet Tri

Hanoi

Hon Gai

Can Pha

Haiphong

LAOS

Thanh Hoa

Gulf of Tonkin

Vinh

THAILAND

Quang Khe

Dong Hoi

Demilitarized Zone

SOUTH VIETNAM

LINEBACKER strikes

LINEBACKER II strikes

Air strikes

Port mining

Main rail line

Main road

N

Note: Linebacker was a U.S. bombing campaign against North Vietnam in May 1972. Linebacker II was a second bombing campaign in December 1972.

0   100 nautical miles

0   100 nautical km

Although many servicemen hated antiwar protesters, by the late 1960s there were more and more friendly contacts between the antiwar movement and the military rank and file. Some grunts in Vietnam wore black armbands on October 15, 1969, to demonstrate their support of the antiwar moratorium. By 1971, 144 underground newspapers had sprung up, directed at soldiers in the United States and overseas, and a dozen or so antiwar coffeehouses were operating near military bases in the United States.

Veterans of the Vietnam War began to play a prominent role in antiwar demonstrations. A new group called Vietnam Veterans Against the War (VVAW) was formed in 1967. From April 19 to 23, 1971, more than 1,000 veterans camped out on the Capitol mall to protest the war, 800 of them tossed combat medals across a fence built to keep them off the Capitol steps. In testimony before the Senate Foreign Relations Committee on April 22, former navy lieutenant (jg) John F. Kerry, a decorated veteran of the Vietnam War and VVAW leader, asked, "How do you ask a man to be the last man to die in Vietnam? How do you ask a man to be the last man to die for a mistake?" (Kerry would be elected U.S. senator from Massachusetts in 1984 and for 2004 seen as a potential Democrat presidential nominee.)

In the spring of 1972 the Communists launched a new offensive, this time equipped with hundreds of Soviet-built T-54 tanks. ARVN forces crumbled in the face of the attack, abandoning 14 bases and the provincial capital of Quang Tri in the north. Nixon responded by resuming air strikes against North Vietnam for the first time since 1968; he also mined Haiphong Harbor. American bombing saved South Vietnam from collapse. At the same time, Nixon continued to promote détente, a policy of peaceful coexistence, with the Communist superpowers, China and the Soviet Union, traveling to both Beijing and Moscow in the winter and spring of 1972. As Lyndon Johnson had demonstrated in 1964, the voters approved when their presidents combined the roles of warrior and peacemaker. Nixon was overwhelmingly reelected in November 1972, defeating the antiwar Democratic challenger, Senator George McGovern.

In Paris, peace negotiations had been continuing since 1969 with virtually no progress. Finally, in the fall of 1972 the basic outlines of an agreement were reached. The Communists dropped their insistence that a new coalition government be set up in South Vietnam as a precondition for peace. The Americans dropped their demand that North Vietnamese troops be withdrawn from the south. The remaining American troops would be pulled out. Henry Kissinger declared that "peace is at hand" shortly before the November election, but Nixon still delayed signing the peace treaty. South Vietnamese president Thieu was unhappy with the treaty, because he believed that it meant South Vietnam was being abandoned by the United States. In fact, the peace agreement left all the important questions about South Vietnam's future unanswered, because there was no room for compromise on such questions.

To reassure Thieu, Nixon rushed more arms shipments to the South Vietnamese government and then launched Operation Linebacker II,

The 1972 Election
"PEACE IS AT HAND"

RICHARD NIXON HAD WON THE WHITE HOUSE IN 1968, promising he had a "secret plan" to end the war in Vietnam. Four years later the war was still being fought; 20,000 more Americans had died in the meantime. The Democratic presidential nominee, South Dakota senator George S. McGovern, hoped to rally antiwar voters into an electoral majority that could deny Nixon his reelection bid.

But Nixon shrewdly sidestepped the challenge. If the war was still raging, he could point to sharply reduced American casualty rates in recent years as evidence that "Vietnamization" was working. His diplomatic triumphs in Beijing and Moscow in the spring of 1972 brought a welcome relaxation of cold war tensions, reducing the chance of war between the nuclear superpowers. Finally, and dramatically, on October 26, 1972, Secretary of State Henry Kissinger announced to a press conference in Washington that the final stumbling blocks to a negotiated settlement of the Vietnam War were removed and "peace was at hand."

But despite Kissinger's optimistic and politically timely announcement, there still was no peace treaty between the United States and North Vietnam. Over the objections of the North Vietnamese, the Nixon administration stalled on signing a final agreement. Nixon did not intend to end the war until he had rushed massive amounts of military aid to the South Vietnamese regime and wrested further concessions from the North Vietnamese at the bargaining table. U.S. bombers continued to hit North Vietnamese targets below the 20th parallel, and Nixon ordered the U.S. Pacific Command to draw up plans for an all-out air assault against North Vietnam, including Hanoi and Haiphong.

None of this mattered (and much of it was not known) to war-weary American voters, who on November 7, 1972, handed Nixon a landslide victory.

the bombing of Hanoi and Haiphong. For 11 days in late December, in what became known as the "Christmas bombing," American planes hit the two cities with the heaviest bombing raids of the war. About 1,500 civilians were killed in the raids, which also caused the destruction of the Bach Mai hospital in Hanoi. Fifteen B-52s and 11 other warplanes were shot down. On the 12th day Nixon halted the bombing and negotiations resumed in Paris.

Although Nixon claimed that the purpose of the bombing had been to force the North Vietnamese back to the bargaining table, in January North Vietnamese and American diplomats agreed to essentially the same terms that had been outlined in October. On January 27, 1973, the Paris peace accords (Agreement on Ending the War and Restoring Peace in Vietnam) were signed, officially ending the war in Vietnam. America's longest war was over, but there were no celebrations in America like the ones that marked the end of World War II. There was no victory in Vietnam, only an armed truce that both sides realized would not last for long.

13
THE WAR ENDS

Richard Nixon defined the U.S. goal in South Vietnam as one of winning "peace with honor." Exactly what that meant was left deliberately vague. In the last year or so of the war, Nixon talked more about securing the release of American POWs than about the future of South Vietnam. The peace accords signed in Paris at the end of January 1973 represented a face-saving device for the United States. Without having to admit defeat, the United States could withdraw its remaining troops from South Vietnam, knowing that there would be at least a "decent interval" before South Vietnam fell to the Communists.

With an estimated 145,000 North Vietnamese troops allowed to remain in South Vietnam, it was obvious that war would soon resume. Without the American military might that had propped it up for a decade and a half, few knowledgeable observers were betting on the long-term survival of the South Vietnam government. Whether Nixon himself fully accepted the likelihood of South Vietnam's defeat after the signing of the peace accords is unclear. He ordered billions of dollars of U.S. military equipment shipped or transferred to the South Vietnamese armed forces, transforming the South Vietnamese air force into the fourth largest in the world. The effect of this continued support was only to delay the inevitable.

As agreed upon in the Paris accords, the North Vietnamese began to release American POWs in February 1973. Five hundred eighty-seven were released by March 29. About 2,500 Americans were officially listed as "missing in action" at the end of the war. By comparison, about 80,000 Americans are still listed as "missing" from World War II and over 8,000 from the Korean War. Many Americans believed that some of

Missing in Action
RAMBO AND AMERICAN MEMORY
OF VIETNAM

EVERY MAJOR U.S. WAR HAS ENDED WITH SOME combatants unaccounted for—"missing in action," or MIA in military terminology. Not every fallen body can be recovered for burial: Pilots die in fiery crashes behind enemy lines, sailors drown, soldiers' bodies are blown apart by high explosives or are buried under muck in rice paddies. There were 80,000 Americans MIA after World War II; 8,000 after the Korean War. Less than 1,200 were listed as MIA at the end of the Vietnam War. None of the nearly 600 American prisoners of war (POWs) who returned from North Vietnam in 1973 claimed that any of their comrades had been left behind, and repeated investigations by the Defense Department and the Senate Select Committee on POW/MIA Affairs turned up no credible evidence that Hanoi still held American prisoners. Nevertheless, many Americans believed, years and decades after the end of the war, that some of the MIAs were in reality still being held in Communist prison camps.

The families of men listed as MIA were understandably reluctant to give up hope that fathers, husbands, brothers, and sons might someday be restored to them. These hopes were sometimes taken advantage of by shady operators, who raised money from gullible donors for "POW rescue missions." Conservative politicians, seeking to block the normalization of diplomatic relations with Vietnam, found the MIA issue useful. Hollywood also shared responsibility for perpetuating the MIA/POW myth, in films like *Missing in Action, Uncommon Valor,* and most famously, Sylvester Stallone's 1985 rescue epic *Rambo: First Blood, Part II.*

Continued popular belief in the existence of the MIA/POWs suggests that for many Americans the war in Vietnam has not come to an end. In that sense, perhaps, Americans still are held captive by Vietnam.

those missing in Vietnam were in reality being held as prisoners by the Communists in Indochina for some unknown purpose years after the war ended. This theory seems unlikely, as reports by the Defense Intelligence Agency have indicated that no American POWs remained in captivity after the spring of 1973.

The returning POWs were regarded by Americans as heroes in a way that most of those returning from their Vietnam duty had not been. If there was any honor involved in Nixon's "peace with honor," it seemed to be provided by the courage and dignity of the POWs. Unlike so many other Americans (both those at home and those who fought in Vietnam), the POWs' faith in the cause that led to their captivity remained bright. Jeremiah Denton, the senior-ranking officer on board the first air force C-141 jet carrying released POWs from Hanoi, read a statement on behalf of his fellow POWs when he stepped off the plane at Clark Air Force Base in the Philippines:

> We are honored to have had the opportunity to serve our country under difficult circumstances. We are profoundly grateful to our Commander-in-Chief and to our Nation for this day. God bless America.

That was not the kind of thing that Americans were accustomed to hearing from the "grunts" when they returned from their year's tour of duty in Vietnam. It was almost as if the POWs—many of whom had been held in captivity since the mid-1960s—were visitors from another, simpler and better age; an era when belief in duty, God, and country was still untarnished by the experience of Vietnam. At the end of World War II, Americans had celebrated the defeat of Germany and Japan. The return of the POWs from German and Japanese captivity had not attracted any special attention. At the end of the Vietnam War there was no U.S. military victory to celebrate. So the return of the POWs from North Vietnamese captivity served as a kind of symbolic substitute victory for many Americans.

The last U.S. troops were pulled out of Vietnam on March 29, 1973, although 8,500 civilian staff and advisers (many of them military men who turned in their uniforms for civilian clothes) remained. American warplanes continued to bomb the communist Khmer Rouge forces in Cambodia until August 1973, when the bombing was forced to an end by a federal court ruling and congressional legislation. Nixon threatened to resume bombing in Vietnam if the North Vietnamese violated the peace settlement, but public and congressional opposition and the deepening Watergate scandal made that a hollow threat.

In 1973 and 1974 Nixon was fighting for his political life. He faced charges that he had obstructed justice by covering up the connections between his reelection campaign and the men arrested for breaking into

THE WAR ENDS

Former American prisoners of war cheer as their aircraft takes off from an airfield near Hanoi as part of Operation Homecoming.
(National Archives)

Democratic Party headquarters in Washington in June 1972. As Congress began considering his impeachment and removal from office, Nixon had less time and less power to do anything on behalf of his ally, South Vietnamese president Nguyen Van Thieu. Congress passed the War Powers Act over Nixon's veto in November 1973, limiting the authority of presidents to commit U.S. troops abroad for longer than two months without congressional approval. And in August 1974 Congress imposed a ceiling of $700 million of military aid to South Vietnam in the coming year. Nixon resigned the presidency that same month as Congress moved toward his impeachment. The new president, Gerald Ford, declared that "our long national nightmare is over." Many Americans took that to be a reference to Vietnam as well as Watergate.

In South Vietnam President Thieu decided that the best defense was a good offense. Violations of the truce began before the ink was dry on the peace accords. Fighting between South and North Vietnamese troops produced tens of thousands of casualties on both sides between 1973 and 1974. Saigon's military forces launched offensives in the spring and summer of 1973 to regain territory from the Communists.

Watergate
HOW THE WAR HELPED DESTROY
THE NIXON PRESIDENCY

NOTHING ENRAGED RICHARD NIXON MORE THAN THE unauthorized "leaking" of information from his administration to the press—particularly any leaks that had to do with the war. In 1970 he authorized the creation of a secret intelligence unit within his administration known as the "plumbers" to undertake investigations of such "leaks." The publication in 1971 of the secret government study of the origins of the Vietnam War known as the Pentagon Papers infuriated Nixon. He made it known to his aides that he wanted information that would help discredit Daniel Ellsberg, the Defense Department consultant who had leaked the Pentagon Papers to the press.

Two "plumbers"—E. Howard Hunt, a former CIA agent, and G. Gordon Liddy, a former FBI agent—were sent to Los Angeles, where they broke into the office of a local psychiatrist, who had Daniel Ellsberg as one of his patients. They failed to turn up anything useful but remained in the president's employment. And in June 1972 they were arrested by Washington, D.C., police for their role in a bungled break-in at the Democratic National Committee headquarters at the Watergate office complex.

The White House denied any involvement in what became known as the Watergate scandal. But investigative reporters from the *Washington Post* and other newspapers came up with financial and other links between Hunt and Liddy and the president's reelection campaign. When the Watergate defendants went to trial in the spring of 1973, the role of the White House in an elaborate cover-up effort began to emerge. The Senate established a committee to investigate the charges, and the Justice Department appointed a special prosecutor to look into the case. Nixon fended off investigators as long as he could, but in August 1974, facing impeachment on charges of obstruction of justice, he resigned from the presidency.

The North Vietnamese, still recovering from their losses in the spring 1972 offensive, laid low for the moment. They stepped up infiltration into the South, turned the Ho Chi Minh trail into a major highway, and built an oil pipeline to fuel their tanks and trucks in the south. They resumed their own offensive in the fall of 1973.

The end came swiftly to South Vietnam, more swiftly than even the North Vietnamese believed possible. As they launched a new offensive in late 1974 they were still thinking of a two-year-long campaign to defeat the Saigon government. In January 1975 the North Vietnamese seized Phuoc Luong province along the Cambodian border. In March 1975 they surrounded and captured the provincial capital Ban Me Thuot in the Central Highlands. President Thieu panicked and ordered

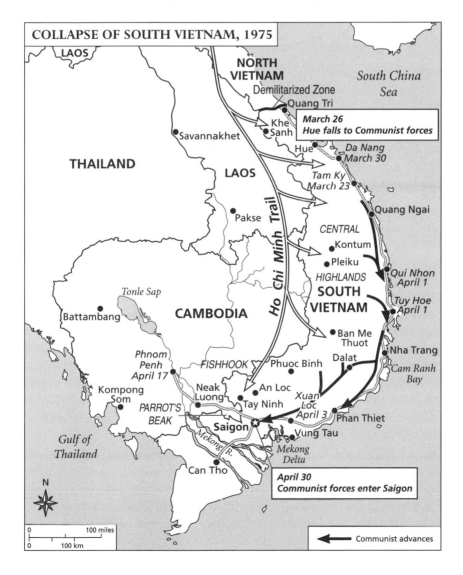

A Corsair II is launched from the nuclear-powered attack aircraft carrier USS *Enterprise* in the South China Sea to provide cover and support for the evacuation of Saigon, April 29, 1975. *(U.S. Navy)*

that ARVN forces withdraw entirely from the Central Highlands and the northern provinces of South Vietnam.

The ARVN retreat turned into a rout. Commanders abandoned their units. Tens of thousands of ARVN soldiers were killed, deserted, or threw away their weapons during the retreat. Half a million refugees jammed the roads. Hue was abandoned to the Communists at the end of March, and Da Nang fell a few days later. The North Vietnam command, realizing that final victory was within its grasp, ordered its armies to press on before ARVN could regroup. By April 1 the Communists controlled more than half of South Vietnam's territory. Thieu resigned the presidency of South Vietnam and fled the country in late April for safety in Taiwan, his suitcases literally filled with gold. He was succeeded in office by Gen. Duong Van Minh ("Big Minh"), who had been hoping to gain power ever since he helped overthrow Diem back in 1963. He would not enjoy it for long. Congress turned down requests from the Ford administration for last-minute funds to aid the lost cause in South Vietnam.

THE WAR ENDS

Graham Martin, who had been appointed U.S. ambassador to Saigon in 1973, delayed giving orders for a general evacuation from Saigon, fearing that it would set off panic in the capital. Martin also was hoping for some last-minute American intervention. The United States did begin an airlift of orphaned Vietnamese children in mid-April, bringing out several thousand before the end of the war. By the end of April, Communist shelling of Tan Son Nhut airport had shut down the possibility of escape by airplane. Order collapsed in Saigon, as embittered South Vietnamese looted U.S. residences and commissaries. Some ARVN soldiers shot at Americans. On April 28 Martin at last agreed to evacuate all Americans from Saigon.

The following day, navy helicopters began Operation Frequent Wind. They carried off 1,000 Americans and about 6,000 Vietnamese to aircraft carriers waiting offshore. Thousands more Vietnamese made their way out to the U.S. fleet on small boats. But tens of thousands of Vietnamese who had worked with the United States, and were likely to be victims of Communist vengeance, were left behind.

Operation Frequent Wind was a strange mixture of calm efficiency and wild disorder. The navy succeeded in its mission to evacuate all the

Vietnamese soldiers and civilians from Saigon await their C-141 journey of evacuation during a stopover in Thailand, April 29, 1975.
(National Archives)

Americans. But the costs were high. As helicopters arrived aboard carriers, they were pushed overboard to make room for more helicopters following them. Two American marines, Cpl. Charles McMahan Jr. and Lance Cpl. Darwin Judge, were killed by an exploding mortar round in the compound of the embassy in Saigon during the evacuation, becoming the last American fatalities of the Vietnam War. At the embassy, marine guards used their rifle butts to beat back desperate Vietnamese trying to get into the embassy and onto helicopters. Alan Carter, a public relations adviser, was one of the last Americans to be evacuated. He later recalled the situation on April 29:

> During the last hours in the embassy there was a sense almost of orderliness. People were doing what they had to do—blowing safes, or destroying files, or sitting and waiting to be taken out. Papers were being put into shredders. And finally, about nine or ten-o'clock, we were told we had better start lining up . . . The chopper flew out around eleven. As we got up in the air a little bit, it was like watching a Roman

Crewmen of the amphibious command ship USS *Blue Ridge* push a Vietnamese H-1 Iroquois helicopter into the South China Sea, April 28, 1975. During evacuation operations for refugees, Vietnamese pilots flew their helicopters to the ship in such large numbers that the copters had to be pushed into the sea to make room for more to land. *(U.S. Navy)*

carnival. Two ammo dumps were going off—one just north of the city, and one at the opposite end. So a lot of stuff was flying around in the air, and it looked like fireworks. There were big crowds around the embassy, and in almost every street you could see people in motion. I remember looking down at this near-orgy of light and firecrackers and thousands of people milling around, and turning to somebody and saying, "Well, there are all those wonderful hearts and minds that we won."

At 7:53 A.M. on April 30, 1975, the last small group of U.S. Marines left in the embassy lowered the American flag and flew to safety.

Later that same morning North Vietnamese tanks rolled up to the front gate of the presidential palace in Saigon and smashed through the ornate iron grill. A soldier unfurled the Viet Cong flag from a balcony of the building. Col. Bui Tin of the North Vietnamese army, a veteran of the war against the French and the siege of Dien Bien Phu, entered the room in the palace where Big Minh awaited him. "I have been waiting since early this morning to transfer power to you," Big Minh told Bui Tin. "There is no question of your transferring power," Bui Tin replied coldly but accurately. "Your power has crumbled. You cannot give up what you do not have." Three decades after Ho Chi Minh had launched his revolution, the Communists were in power throughout Vietnam. Saigon would be renamed Ho Chi Minh City to mark the Communist victory.

In neighboring Cambodia the Communists had already come to power in mid-April; in Laos they would control the country by December. The last U.S. military action in Indochina came a week and a half after the fall of Saigon. The Cambodian Khmer Rouge seized a U.S. merchant ship, the *Mayaguez,* on May 12, and briefly held its 39 seamen. President Ford ordered a sea and air attack on Cambodia on May 14 in response. Forty-one marines were killed in the attack. The crew of the *Mayaguez* was actually in the process of being released when U.S. planes attacked. Although the attack proved unnecessary and cost more lives than it might have saved, President Ford's popularity soared afterward. Like the release of the POWs and the airlift of Vietnamese orphans, the "rescue" of the *Mayaguez* crew helped Americans ignore the greater failure of the war they had fought in Vietnam.

"We have regained tranquility for ten thousand generations," the Vietnamese poet Nguyen Trai wrote in the 15th century, after the defeat of Chinese invaders. It did not prove an accurate prophecy in either the 15th or the 20th century. Vietnam remained an unhappy land. Officially reunited in 1976 as the Socialist Republic of Vietnam, the country suffered from the economic consequences of 30 years of war and poor economic planning by its Communist rulers. Although no "bloodbath" took place in Vietnam comparable to that in neighboring Cambodia under the Khmer Rouge, the Vietnamese Communists did imprison tens of thousands of former soldiers and supporters of the Saigon government in "reeducation camps." The Vietnamese would soon be at war again, this time against their former allies the Khmer Rouge and the Chinese Communists. Poverty, political repression, and war drove some 1.5 million refugees out of Vietnam in the decade after the end of the war. They became known as "boat people" because so many of them set out for exile in small and often unseaworthy boats. Some of the refugees spent years in camps in Thailand, Hong Kong, and elsewhere in Southeast Asia. Others, more fortunate, were able to find permanent homes

In the South China Sea, a small boat carrying Vietnamese refugees is pulled alongside the guided-missile destroyer USS *Towers* during rescue operations. *(U.S. Navy)*

in new lands. Some 725,000 Vietnamese settled in the United States after the war, sometimes finding material prosperity but still missing their homeland.

It will be many generations before Vietnam recovers from the effects of the war. The South Vietnamese armed forces lost nearly 200,000 killed. The number of Viet Cong and North Vietnamese dead lay somewhere between half a million and a million. A million or more civilians were also killed. All told, at least one-tenth of the population of Vietnam was killed or wounded in the war. The land itself was scarred by the conflict. Vietnam's landscape is covered with bomb craters, its rivers and forests are still poisoned by the residue of Agent Orange and other American pesticides, and farmers are still being killed when they accidentally plow up unexploded bombs, artillery shells, and mines.

In the United States, the costs of the war are also still felt. In Vietnam 47,244 Americans were killed in battle, and 10,446 others died from related causes such as accidents and disease, a total of more than 57,000. Over 300,000 more were wounded, some maimed for life. Thousands of other veterans have suffered from post-traumatic stress disorder (which in earlier wars was called "battle fatigue" or "shell shock"), from the effects of exposure to Agent Orange, or from drug addiction related to their service in Vietnam. Economically, the United States also paid a heavy price for the Vietnam War. The war cost the United States $150 billion in direct expenses and billions more every year in veterans' benefits. And the war set off a wave of inflation in the late 1960s that weakened the economy for a decade afterward.

Many of the veterans who served in Vietnam put the war behind them after they returned to the United States. But for many others the war continued to poison their lives. Unlike the end of World War II, there were no big victory parades for the troops returning from Vietnam. Instead of whole units coming back together, Vietnam veterans returned as individuals when their year-long "tour of duty" ran out. A few veterans were spit upon or called "baby-killers" when they returned. Steven Gist, who served with the marines in Vietnam in 1967, had a more pleasant reception when he stepped off the plane in Los Angeles in January 1968. Somebody bought him a drink at the bar. "I was never spit on," he recalled:

> I was never spat at. I never have talked to any other vet who was. Someone always claims to know someone else who was—and always at

the airport. Like most other things concerning Vietnam, I think it was probably blown out of proportion. Most people really just didn't give a damn whether you were there or not, and I think most people still don't.

But that was part of the problem; nobody "gave a damn." Vietnam veterans felt neglected compared to veterans of other wars, unhonored by their country after they had risked their lives and seen their friends killed in a distant, unpopular war. Recognition finally came to the vets when the Vietnam memorial was dedicated in Washington, D.C., in 1982. The memorial consists of two long polished black granite walls bearing the name of every U.S. serviceman who died in Vietnam. Although some veterans' groups initially criticized the memorial for not being heroic enough in design, it has become one of the most visited and most moving monuments in the nation's capital.

Vietnam was America's most divisive war while it was being fought, and it remains a source of debate and division years after the fall of Saigon. For some, like former president Ronald Reagan, it was a "noble war," spoiled only by the unwillingness of civilian leaders to allow the military to go in and do what was necessary for victory. For others, Vietnam was a lost cause from the beginning, an object lesson in national arrogance, bureaucratic self-deception, and moral callousness.

In the end, Vietnam was a futile war that caused a great deal of suffering and that nobody won. Morley Safer, who served as a CBS correspondent in Vietnam in the mid-1960s and early 1970s, revisited the country in 1989 for the first time since the war. He spent one day in the company of a man named Nguyen Ngoc Hung, an English teacher in Hanoi who in 1968 at the age of 18 was drafted by the North Vietnamese army and sent to fight in the south. He had no great desire to be a soldier, but when forced to fight he did his duty bravely. On the trek southward along the Ho Chi Minh trail, American B-52s bombed his company. Two of his friends were killed. "After the B-52 raids," he recalled as if it were yesterday, "you go around and gather up the bits, the pieces of the bodies, and you try to bury them." Hung drove with Safer to a military cemetery near Quang Tri where the bodies of 10,000 Communist soldiers lay buried. Earlier in Hanoi, Safer had asked Hung who had won the war. Now, walking back to their car, Hung thought out loud:

At first we thought we won the war . . . but I look at this place and I realize we did not. It was something like fighting with somebody in your house with all the precious furniture around you. And after the stranger leaves, you look at the different things in your house. And they are all broken. The war actually took place in our house. It was a very sad thing. Think about it . . . after all that war, we haven't been able to change you, and you haven't been able to change us.

"The Wall"

SINCE ITS DEDICATION ON VETERANS DAY 1982, THE Vietnam Veterans Memorial has been one of the most popular sites for visitors in Washington, D.C. Better known simply as "the Wall," the memorial consists of a 500-foot-long V-shaped rampart of black granite, seemingly dug into the landscape between the Washington and Lincoln Memorials. Its 140 panels bear the names of the more than 58,000 U.S. servicemen and women who lost their lives in the Vietnam War between 1959 and 1975. Although its designer had no way of knowing this would happen, the Vietnam Veterans Memorial became a place where ordinary Americans have joined in an ongoing and ever-changing display of sorrow and remembrance. People leave daily offerings before the names of loved ones and former comrades-in-arms, ranging from baby pictures to military medals to cans of beer. As former Vietnam War correspondent Arnold Isaacs noted in his 1997 book, *Vietnam Shadows,* "No one leaves notes or offerings at the rest of Washington's many monuments."

Although located on federal land, the cost of construction of the Vietnam Veterans Memorial was borne entirely by private donations. Fourteen hundred designs were submitted for the memorial: The winning design was from a 21-year-old architecture student at Yale University named Maya Lin. Her plan was not immediately or universally popular. Some veterans saw her somber memorial as an insult to veterans, a "black gash of shame" that bore little resemblance to more traditional representations of America's fighting men, like the Iwo Jima flag-raising statue in Arlington National Cemetery that commemorates a World War II victory. But in the end, most of the dissenters were won over, coming to see the beauty of Lin's vision of the Wall as a place where the living and the dead would meet again, in her words, "between the sunny world and the quiet dark world beyond."

The Vietnam War Memorial, its long walls of black granite inscribed with the names of more than 50,000 war fatalities *(W. Clark, National Park Service, U.S. Department of the Interior)*

The United States was spared the physical destruction that shattered Vietnam in the 1960s and 1970s. But Americans suffered the pain and humiliation of their first military defeat, and many still are struggling to come to grips with the meaning of the Vietnam War.

Glossary

Agent Orange   A powerful herbicide that was sprayed from low-flying U.S. airplanes to kill off the vegetation claimed to be hiding the enemy; its name came from the color of the large barrels in which it was stored. It contains a poisonous chemical labeled 2,4,5-T, a form of dioxin, which in the years since has been linked to a number of medical problems suffered by those exposed to Agent Orange.

airborne   People or material delivered by helicopters or other aircraft.

aircraft carrier   A warship equipped with a deck for the taking off and landing of aircraft, and storage space for the aircraft.

AK-47   A Russian and Chinese assault rifle used extensively by Communist forces in Vietnam.

ammunition   The materials used in discharging firearms or any weapon that throws projectiles, including powder, shot, shrapnel, bullets, cartridges, and the means of igniting and exploding them, such as primers and fuses. Bombs, grenades, and mines are also ammunition; projectiles carrying nuclear, biological, and chemical devices are now also ammunition; certain rockets and missiles may also be regarded as ammunition.

amphibious warfare   The delivery of armed forces from shipboard to a hostile shoreline by waterborne craft.

appeasement   The act of acceding to the belligerent demands of a group or country, usually involving a sacrifice of principle or justice.

ARVN (Army of the Republic of Viet Nam)   The South Vietnamese armed forces.

atrocity   A criminal act carried out by members of a military unit in wartime, such as the murder of unarmed civilians.

attrition Wearing down enemy resources and ability to continue armed conflict, as when military attacks are launched not primarily to take ground but to kill as many of an opponent's people as possible.

bazooka A cylindrical rocket launcher carried by infantry in World War II. It fired a projectile intended to penetrate the armor plating of a tank or other military vehicle.

body count A system employed by the U.S. military to measure progress in the war against communism in South Vietnam by keeping track of enemy casualties.

booby traps Explosives or other devices concealed in objects or locations that unsuspecting soldiers might trigger by their movements or actions.

casualties Losses of military personnel to enemy action. When reported of battles, these usually include those killed, wounded, captured, or missing in action. When reported for an entire war, casualties may also include those who die in noncombat activities and from diseases contracted while in theaters of war. Civilian casualties are reported separately.

civil war A war between parties, regions, or ethnic groups within a single country.

coalition A combination or alliance arranged on a temporary basis, as among wartime allies.

collective security A policy or principle in international affairs, according to which many countries band together to guarantee the security of individual countries against foreign aggression.

colonialism A system under which one people or territory are ruled from afar by another country.

communism The theory and system of social organization that is based on common or state ownership of industry, agriculture, and all other economic enterprises; a system of government based upon the dictatorship of the Communist Party.

convoy A group of ships or land vehicles traveling together for mutual protection, sometimes under armed escort.

counterinsurgency The guiding doctrine of U.S. military involvement in South Vietnam in the early 1960s, emphasizing mobility and surprise by small units of highly trained combat specialists, as well as "winning the hearts and minds" of the civilian population.

coup (coup d'état) The overthrow of an established government through an unexpected and rapid takeover by a small group of plotters. *Coup* is the French word for a forceful blow and is sometimes used with the complete French term, *coup d'état,* an overthrow of the government.

covert Undercover or secret. When used in a wartime context, it applies to usually small-scale operations that may be conducted by either the military or civilians.

defoliants Chemical agents used to wither or kill off vegetation, to deny cover to enemy forces operating in jungles and forests.

delta A flat fertile ground between the diverging branches of a river system, where the river empties into a larger body of water such as the sea.

dogfight An aerial battle between opposing fighter pilots.

domino theory The belief, first enunciated by President Eisenhower, that if South Vietnam fell to the Communists it would trigger a series of Communist takeovers through Asia and perhaps beyond, like a row of dominoes toppling over in sequence.

draft Involuntary military recruitment through the selection of individuals from the civilian population to join a nation's armed forces.

draft resistance The refusal by individuals or organized groups to cooperate with the draft system.

fragging Military slang for the deliberate killing of a superior officer by men of lower rank in the same army. The word is derived from *fragmentation grenade,* which is often used for this purpose.

free-fire zone A territory considered to be under enemy control, where any person, vehicle, or structure is considered a legitimate military target.

friendly fire Combat deaths or wounds caused by the guns, bombs, or artillery of one's own side in a war.

Green Berets Nickname for U.S. Army Special Forces soldiers, trained in counterinsurgency techniques. It derives from their distinctive headgear.

grunt Popular nickname for U.S. Army and Marine Corps ground combat forces in South Vietnam.

guerrilla warfare A strategy of warfare in which small bands of nonuniformed soldiers harass a larger and better-armed enemy through surprise raids or attacks on supply and communication lines, and usually depending on the sympathy of local civilians for information and shelter.

helicopters Rotary-winged aircraft capable of vertical take-offs and landings; used extensively by the United States in the Vietnam War.

herbicide Chemical agent used to wither or kill off vegetation for the purpose of denying cover to the enemy, or to destroy enemy food crops.

infiltration A method of attack in which small units of troops penetrate enemy lines through weak or unguarded points.

kill ratio The proportion of enemy to friendly forces killed in a given battle or campaign.

logistics The branch of military science concerned with the transportation and supply of troops in the field.

M-16 From 1966 on, the standard-issue automatic weapon used by U.S. forces in Vietnam.

machine gun A small weapon able to deliver a rapid and continuous fire of bullets until the weapon's magazine or firing belt is depleted.

MIA (missing in action) Military personnel whose fate is unaccounted for after a battle, not known to authorities to have been either killed or captured.

mine A device containing an explosive charge, placed in a camouflaged setting, and designed to explode and kill enemy soldiers or destroy enemy vehicles when they are in its immediate vicinity.

missionaries Religious believers, often members of the clergy, who travel to distant lands to convert others to their religion.

morphine A narcotic derived from opium, which when inserted into the bloodstream can dull pain or induce unconsciousness.

mortar A relatively small, portable cannon, loaded in the muzzle, that fires its shells at a slow speed and short range but with a high, arching trajectory.

napalm An incendiary weapon made of jellied gasoline, dropped from aircraft in canisters or fired from flame-throwers, used by U.S. troops in Vietnam.

nationalism Devotion to the interests of one's own nation, including the desire for national independence.

neutrality The status of a nation that does not participate in a war.

New Left Campus-based radicals in the 1960s, active in the antiwar, civil rights, and feminist movements. The "new" was applied to distinguish them from the previous generation's leftists and their agenda.

pacification   The process by which a government extends its influence in a region controlled by enemy insurgents.

pacifist   An opponent of war on the principle of opposition to killing.

POW (prisoner of war)   Military personnel taken captive and being held by the enemy.

propaganda   News and commentary on news released by a government in wartime and intended to persuade domestic and foreign audiences of the righteousness of the government's cause.

quartermaster   Military officer charged with providing shelter, clothing, provisions, fuel, and other materials to troops in the field.

rear echelon   That part of a military force in the field that does not serve in combat in the front lines, but rather provides command structure, services, and material to the soldiers at the front.

reconnaissance   A search for useful military information in the field made by means of observation of enemy positions and movements, and the physical landscape upon which battles are likely to occur.

reprisal   The infliction of injury on an enemy in warfare in retaliation for an injury suffered at the enemy's hands.

rice paddy   A flooded field used for the cultivation of rice.

sortie   The flight of an individual aircraft on a combat mission.

supply dump   A place where a large quantity of military materials, including ammunition, fuel, or food, has been gathered prior to distribution to soldiers in the field.

Tet   The Vietnamese lunar new year, a major holiday. It comes in January and is observed for several days.

torpedo   A self-propelled explosive device, launched from a submarine, boat, or airplane and designed to travel underwater and sink an enemy ship.

Viet Cong (National Liberation Front)   South Vietnamese slang name for the Communist ("Cong") guerrilla movement in South Vietnam, officially known as the National Liberation Front.

Vietnamization   Term coined by the Nixon administration for the policy of withdrawing U.S. ground combat forces from South Vietnam, while turning over responsibility for fighting to the South Vietnamese military.

Further Reading

NONFICTION

Appy, Christian G. *Working-Class War.* Chapel Hill: University of North Carolina Press, 1993.

Baritz, Loren. *Backfire: A History of How American Culture Led Us into Vietnam and Made Us Fight the Way We Did.* New York: William Morrow, 1985.

Barrett, David M. *Uncertain Warriors: Lyndon Johnson and His Vietnam Advisers.* Lawrence: University of Kansas Press, 1993.

Beattie, Keith. *The Scar That Binds: American Culture and the Vietnam War.* New York: New York University Press, 1998.

Beschloss, Michael R. *Taking Charge: The Johnson White House Tapes, 1963–1964.* New York: Simon and Schuster, 1997.

Bird, Kai. *The Color of Truth: McGeorge and William Bundy: Brothers in Arms.* New York: Simon and Schuster, 1998.

Boettcher, Thomas D. *Vietnam: The Valor and the Sorrow.* Boston: Little, Brown, 1985.

Bradley, Mark Philip. *Imagining Vietnam and America: The Making of a Postcolonial Vietnam, 1919–1950.* Chapel Hill: University of North Carolina Press, 2000.

Braestrup, Peter. *Big Story: How the American Press and Television Reported and Interpreted the Crisis of Tet 1968 in Vietnam and Washington.* New Haven, Conn.: Yale University Press, 1977.

Brands, H. W. *The Wages of Globalism: Lyndon Johnson and the Limits of American Power.* New York: Oxford University Press, 1996.

Brigham, Robert K. *Guerrilla Diplomacy: The NLF's Foreign Relations and the Viet Nam War.* Ithaca, N.Y.: Cornell University Press, 1999.

Broyles, William. *Brothers in Arms: A Journey from War to Peace.* New York: Knopf, 1986.

Bundy, William. *A Tangled Web: The Making of Foreign Policy in the Nixon Presidency.* New York: Hill and Wang, 1998.

Buzzanco, Robert. *Masters of War: Military Dissent and Politics in the Vietnam Era.* New York: Cambridge University Press, 1996.

Cable, Larry. *Conflict of Myths: The Development of American Counterinsurgency Doctrine and the Vietnam War.* New York: New York University Press, 1988.

Carhart, Tom. *Battlefront Vietnam.* New York: Warner Books, 1991.

———. *The Offering.* New York: William Morrow, 1987.

Caputo, Philip. *A Rumor of War.* New York: Owlet, 1996.

Dean, Eric T. *Shook Over Hell: Post-Traumatic Stress, Vietnam and the Civil War.* Cambridge, Mass.: Harvard University Press, 1997.

Doyle, Robert C. *Voices from Captivity: Interpreting the American POW Narrative.* Lawrence: University Press of Kansas, 1994.

Duiker, William J. *Ho Chi Minh.* New York: Hyperion, 2000.

Edelman, Bernard, ed. *Dear America: Letters Home from Vietnam.* New York: Simon and Schuster, 1985.

Elliott, Duong Van Mai. *Sacred Willow: Four Generations in the Life of a Vietnamese Family.* New York: Oxford University Press, 1999.

Erhart, W. D. *Passing Time.* Jefferson, N.C.: McFarland, 1989.

Franklin, Bruce. *MIA, or Mythmaking in America.* Rev. ed. New Brunswick, N.J.: Rutgers University Press, 1993.

Gaiduk, Ilya V. *The Soviet Union and the Vietnam War.* Chicago: Ivan R. Dee, 1996.

Gardner, Lloyd C. *Pay Any Price: Lyndon Johnson and the Wars for Vietnam.* Chicago: Ivan R. Dee, 1995.

Generous, Kevin M. *Vietnam: The Secret War.* New York: Gallery Books, 1985.

Gioglio, Gerald R. *Days of Decision: An Oral History of Conscientious Objectors in the Military During the Vietnam War.* Trenton, N.J.: Broken Rifle Press, 1989.

Grant, Zalin. *Survivors: Vietnam POWs Tell Their Stories.* New York: Da Capo Press, 1994.

Halberstam, David. *The Best and the Brightest.* New York: Random House, 1972.

Hammond, William M. *Reporting Vietnam: Media and Military at War.* Lawrence: University Press of Kansas, 1998.

Hass, Kristin Ann. *Carried to the Wall: American Memory and the Vietnam Veterans Memorial.* Berkeley: University of California Press, 1998.

Hendrickson, Paul. *The Living and the Dead: Robert McNamara and Five Lives of a Lost War.* New York: Alfred A. Knopf, 1996.

Herr, Michael. *Dispatches.* New York: Alfred A. Knopf, 1978.

Herring, George C. *America's Longest War: The United States and Vietnam, 1950–1975.* New York: Alfred A. Knopf, 1978.

———. *LBJ and Vietnam: A Different Kind of War.* Austin: University of Texas Press, 1994.

Howes, Craig. *Voices of the Vietnam POWs: Witnesses to Their Fight.* New York: Oxford University Press, 1993.

Hunt, Michael H. *Lyndon Johnson's War: America's Cold War Crusade in Vietnam, 1945–1968: A Critical Issue.* New York: Hill and Wang, 1996.

Kahin, George M. *Intervention: How America Became Involved in Vietnam.* New York: Alfred A. Knopf, 1986.

Karnow, Stanley. *Vietnam: A History.* New York: Viking, 1983.

Keating, Susan Katz. *Prisoners of Hope: Exploiting the POW/MIA Myth in America.* New York: Random House, 1994.

Kimball, Jeffrey. *Nixon's Vietnam War.* Lawrence: University of Kansas Press, 1998.

Kovic, Ron. *Born on the Fourth of July.* New York: Simon and Schuster, 1976.

Langguth, A. J. *Our Vietnam: The War, 1945–1975.* New York: Simon and Schuster, 2000.

Lanning, Michael L. *Vietnam at the Movies.* New York: Fawcett Columbine, 1994.

Lawrence, Mark A. *Selling Vietnam: The European Colonial Powers and the Origins of the American Commitment to Vietnam, 1944–1950.* Berkeley: University of California Press, 2002.

Lembcke, Jerry. *The Spitting Image: Myth, Memory and the Legacy of Vietnam.* New York: New York University Press, 1998.

Lewy, Guenter. *America in Vietnam: Illusion, Myth and Reality.* New York: Oxford University Press, 1978.

Logevall, Fredrik. *Choosing War: The Lost Chance for Peace and the Escalation of War in Vietnam.* Berkeley: University of California Press, 1999.

Marr, David. *Vietnam 1945: The Quest for Power.* Berkeley: University of California Press, 1995.

Martin, Andrew. *Receptions of War: Vietnam in American Culture.* Norman: University of Oklahoma Press, 1993.

Maurer, Harry. *Strange Ground: Americans in Vietnam: 1945–1975, An Oral History.* New York: Henry Holt, 1989.

McConnell, Malcolm. *Inside Hanoi's Secret Archives: Solving the MIA Mystery.* New York: Simon & Schuster, 1995.

McNamara, Robert. *In Retrospect: The Tragedy and Lessons of Vietnam.* New York: Times Books, 1995.

McNamara, Robert S., James Blight, and Robert Brigham. *Argument Without End: In Search of Answers to the Vietnam Tragedy.* New York: Public Affairs, 1999.

Morris, Stephen J. *Why Vietnam Invaded Cambodia: Political Culture and the Causes of War.* Stanford, Calif.: Stanford University Press, 1999.

Moser, Richard. *The New Winter Soldiers: GI and Veteran Dissent During the Vietnam Era.* New Brunswick, N.J.: Rutgers University Press, 1996.

Nixon, Richard. *No More Vietnams.* New York: Arbor House, 1985.

Oberdorfer, Don. *Tet!* New York: Doubleday, 1971.

Page, Tim, et al. *Another War: Pictures of the War from the Other Side*. Washington, D.C.: National Geographic Society, 2002.

Palmer, Bruce. *The 25-Year War: America's Military Role in Vietnam*. Lexington: University of Kentucky Press, 1984.

Palmer, Laura. *Shrapnel in the Heart: Letters and Remembrances from the Vietnam Veterans Memorial*. New York: Random House, 1987.

Possony, Stefan. *Aggression and Self-Defense: The Legality of U.S. Action in South Vietnam*. Philadelphia: University of Pennsylvania, Foreign Policy Research Institute, 1966.

Qiang Zhai. *China and the Vietnam Wars, 1950–1975*. Chapel Hill: University of North Carolina Press, 2000.

Record, Jeffrey. *The Wrong War: Why We Lost in Vietnam*. Annapolis, Md.: Naval Institute Press, 1998.

Reporting Vietnam: American Journalism, 1954–1971. New York: Library of America, 2000.

Safer, Morley. *Flashbacks: On Returning to Vietnam*. New York: Random House, 1990.

Schulzimer, Robert D. *The United States and Vietnam, 1941–1975*. New York: Oxford University Press, 1997.

Sheehan, Neil. *A Bright Shining Lie: John Paul Vann and America in Vietnam*. New York: Random House, 1988.

Summers, Harry G. *On Strategy: A Critical Analysis of the Vietnam War*. Novato, Calif.: Presidio Press, 1982.

Summers, Harry G., and Stanley Karnow. *Historical Atlas of the Vietnam War*. Boston: Houghton Mifflin, 1996.

Terry, Wallace. *Bloods: An Oral History of the Vietnam War by Black Veterans*. New York: Ballantine Books, 1984.

Tripp, Nathaniel. *Father, Soldier, Son: Memoir of a Platoon Leader in Vietnam*. South Royalton, Vt.: Steerforth Press, 1996.

Walker, Keith. *A Piece of My Heart: The Stories of Twenty-Six American Women Who Served in Vietnam*. New York: Ballantine Books, 1985.

Wells, Tom. *The War Within: America's Battle over Vietnam*. Berkeley: University of California Press, 1994.

Young, Marilyn. *The Vietnam Wars, 1945–1990*. New York: Ballantine Books, 1985.

Zaroulis, Nancy, and Sullivan, Gerald. *Who Spoke Up? American Protest Against the War in Vietnam, 1963–1975*. Garden City, N.Y.: Doubleday, 1984.

FICTION

Del Vecchio, John. *The 13th Valley*. New York: Bantam Books, 1982.

Glick, Allen. *Winters Coming, Winters Gone*. New York: Pinnacle Books, 1985.

Karlin, Wayne. *Lost Armies*. New York: Henry Holt, 1988.

Mason, Bobbie Ann. *In Country.* New York: Harper and Row, 1985.
O'Brien, Tim. *Going after Cacciato.* New York: Delacorte Press, 1978.

WEBSITES

Battlefield: Vietnam. Available online. URL: http://www.pbs.org/battlefield-vietnam/. Downloaded on March 27, 2002.
Vietnam War Internet Project. Available online. URL: http://www.vwip.org/vwiphome.html. Downloaded on March 27, 2002.
Vietnam: Yesterday and Today. Available online. URL: http://servercc.oakton.edu/~wittman/. Downloaded on March 27, 2002.
"The Wars for Viet Nam: 1945 to 1975," Vassar College Website. Available online. URL: http://vietnam.vassar.edu. Downloaded on March 27, 2002.

Index

Page numbers in *italics* indicate a photograph. Page numbers
followed by *m* indicate maps. Page numbers followed by *g* indicate glossary
entries. Page numbers in **boldface** indicate box features.

171

INDEX

INDEX

177

INDEX

INDEX